# LOVERS ROCK

# LOVERS ROCK:
## Let The Music Play

Hartley Hines

*Copyright © 2015 by Hartley Hines*
*E-Book edition*

All rights reserved. No part of this publication may be reproduced or transmitted in any form or by any means,electronic or mechanical, including photocopying, recording, or any other information storage and retrieval system, without the written permission of the publisher.

This is a completely fictitious story, which includes the names of some real people who are in the public domain. All other characters with any resemblance to actual persons, living or dead, is entirely coincidental.

Hyperlinks to third party websites (i.e. YouTube) are accessed at your own risk. The publishers or suppliers of this E-book cannot be held liable for any content displayed nor any failure of content to display.

ISBN-13: 978-1507888179 (For print reference only)
ISBN-10: 1507888171(For print reference only)

Contact: hartleyhines@gmail.com

# Book Review

Reviewer: Glenville Ashby, PhD

A Soulful Novel

Author Hartley Hines takes a sanguine look at affairs of the heart. With sheer craft he uses the power of music to reflect our innermost sentiments. Throughout we are served with the titles of songs that capture the thoughts and feelings of those in love. Songs of joy, pain, angst, wistfulness and ecstasy are internalized and channelled by Hines' characters. For example, when Dennis, a heartthrob of a singer falls for Sonia, a designer, their desires are immortalized in music. Hines writes, "One of his most heartfelt poems extolled his admiration for her from the very first time he had blessed his eyes on her, when he pictured her to be his bride. He must have been listening to a song called "I Admire You" (Roland &. Carolyn) because those sentiments are conveyed in the lyrics."

Lovers Rock is a soulful novel, really, a rhythmic dance of personalities. While Dennis wears his affection on his sleeve, Sonia fiercely shields her independence. But sometimes this can be risky; and riskier still is her tangential attitude toward Dennis when he first laid bare his emotions.

Hines explains, "Sonia did not mean to start turning her back on Dennis, the one person she had ever loved, but in her head there were unresolved issues of jealousy which she had to deal with. She was sure it could all be sorted in time, but there were also many distractions in her new life in England..."

With Sonia leaving Jamaica to pursue studies in England, their relationship buckles under the weight of separation. Meanwhile,

Dennis' career as a musician soars, even capturing the attention of a revered legend. Young women are bowled over by his vocal range and physical appeal, making Sonia's nonchalance that more perplexing.

But providence steps in. When Sonia's gran passes she reunites with Dennis for the funerary occasion. They also attend an engagement party during her sojourn. It is time to share memories and rekindle family ties. There is nostalgia and the love of country. Dennis poses the intriguing subject of permanently returning to Jamaica. While others opt for careers over nationhood, Dennis responds that 'no matter where he goes or what he does, he knows he will always be coming home to his island.'

But the magnetic draw of the island proves overwhelmingly compelling. And so is the power of love. Sonia decides to stay with Dennis in their native land but she must first return to England to tie loose ends. Other family members follow suit.

Ever present is a tale of a silver bangle, a family heirloom given to Sonia by her deceased gran, but there's little information on the whereabouts of its accompanying piece.

Remarkably it shows up in an African antique shop and later discovered by Sonia during a romantic stroll with Dennis along a London street. The history behind the bangle rivals the most legendary of tales. It is wrapped in African royalty, the transatlantic slave trade, slavery, and forbidden love. Now in their possession, the bangles are more than a testament of love. It seals their love till the end of time.

Lovers Rock is written with an unmistakable joie de vivre. In a world on tenterhooks, Hines' work proves a fitting antidote. In this warm narrative, hearts flutter with amorous expectations, old flames rekindle, and hopes are dashed only to be revived. Love is portrayed on a clean slate unsullied by lustful overreach.

As if riding on the soaring vocals and gravitas of the leading character we are nostalgic and not surprisingly quite smitten.

Feedback: glenvilleashby@gmail.com or follow him on Twitter@glenvilleashby

# DEDICATION

Dedicated to my dad. Rest in peace 'Man Cool.'

## TABLE OF CONTENTS

| | | |
|---|---|---|
| CHAPTER 1 | Time To Leave | 13 |
| CHAPTER 2 | England Calling | 29 |
| CHAPTER 3 | The Grovans | 33 |
| CHAPTER 4 | Back A Yard | 43 |
| CHAPTER 5 | Games People Play | 51 |
| CHAPTER 6 | Forget Me Not | 59 |
| CHAPTER 7 | Hello Stranger | 67 |
| CHAPTER 8 | The Day Trip | 77 |
| CHAPTER 9 | Kingston Town | 83 |
| CHAPTER 10 | Engagement Party | 95 |
| CHAPTER 11 | Goodbye Granny | 103 |
| CHAPTER 12 | Returning Residents | 111 |
| CHAPTER 13 | Two Will Always Be One | 117 |
| CHAPTER 14 | Dance Cruel | 127 |
| CHAPTER 15 | Double Trouble | 141 |
| CHAPTER 16 | This Is Lovers Rock | 149 |
| Epilogue | | 155 |
| Lovers Rock 2 | | 169 |

| | |
|---|---|
| Song List | 170 |
| Other Books By Author | 173 |
| About The Author | 174 |

# INTRODUCTION

Created in the UK, the genre of music termed Lovers Rock has its roots firmly in Jamaica, reggae's originating home. In fact some classic Jamaican reggae love songs are included in this story, which is dedicated to all who know what Lovers Rock was, what Lovers Rock is, and what Lovers Rock will always be; an infectious musical bug that, once caught, never leaves you.

Of course, 43 of these songs could never hope to fully give justice to the enormous amount of Lovers Rock songs out there. However, readers can view this small slice as an introduction to Lovers Rock, from which they can go out and discover more for themselves.

Most of the chosen songs have lyrical relevance to the storyline, which takes you from the hot tropical island of Jamaica to the not so sunny UK shores.

When she leaves Jamaica for England, will Sonia remember her boyfriend, Dennis, whom she promised would be her boy for life? And can she trust him to stay loyal despite being a member of an immensely popular three boy reggae band? In addition to all of this, what significance does an African heirloom have in both their lives?

You are sure to enjoy this intriguing story that is held together so wonderfully by the featured classic Lovers Rock songs. Listen to the soundtrack, as you read the book, on my YouTube playlist: <u>Lovers Rock Let The Music Play</u>

So, let the music play, and enjoy...

# CHAPTER 1
## TIME TO LEAVE

On the beautiful Caribbean island of Jamaica, in the month of January 1976, an attractive teenage girl, named Sonia, was preparing to leave that sun-drenched land of wood and water. Her parents, who had left her living with her grandparents for just over eight years, had finally sent for her to join them in England.

Sonia's maternal grandparents, Rensford and Miriam Henderson, were proud to have raised five children of their own; two boys and three girls, in a home that was filled with warmth and love. Two of their daughters, Ethel and Valerie, were residing in the

United States, while Sonia's mother, Sandra, their eldest daughter, lived in England. Their two sons were, Marcus, the youngest and last child, who lived in Canada, and George, the eldest of the five, who also lived in England. Between the five of them, they had left eight grandchildren behind, over the years when they had gone abroad to better themselves, certain of sending for them later. Normally, after a few years of working hard and finding suitable accommodation, they would arrange for their children to join them.

Miriam, affectionately known to everyone as granny Henni, together with Rensford, had enjoyed the temporary task of looking after those grandchildren. And so it was that one by one they had all departed, and by 1975 only Sonia and Patsy remained. Patsy was George's daughter who would be leaving in that year too.

The sleepy village of Grovan Pen, where they lived, was a humble farming community situated a few miles west of Morant Bay, the capital town of the eastern parish of St Thomas. Their bungalow home was a typical dwelling, built in a style often seen around the island, with verandas to both the front and back. Over the years there had been a few rooms added on to accommodate family members when visiting from abroad.

Twice each week in the large and very popular covered market in Morant Bay, granny Henni ran a little stall on which she sold a selection of ladies underwear and bars of soap. She got her supplies from various wholesalers in the local area; but at times she'd go as far as Port Antonio, when she knew there was a good sale on. It did not make a great deal of money, but she liked the freedom it gave her to get out of the house and meet different folk. Sometimes she took one or two of the youngsters with her to help with the stall during school holidays. This was something she had done when her own children were young too. The little ones always loved to help out at the market; not least because she would treat them to beef patties, followed by bulla cakes and cherry malt box drinks for lunch. On her return from the market, Rensford usually had a nice meal prepared for the family. His delicious cooking was eagerly anticipated by everyone, and when he got praised for it, he always said unassumingly, "Thank the Lord and thank the hand," which usually raised a smile from all who heard it.

Rensford had been a rock to his wife, for over fifty four years of marriage, until his untimely death in 1971, which was caused from complications brought on by diabetes. Ever since he died, a day did not pass without Henni thinking about him dearly. Just a glance around the house would trigger memories of his handiwork and how he had maintained it so well, always making sure the outside paintwork looked fresh and colourful.

After his death, Henni had often enlisted the help of Aaron, a friendly neighbour, to do any maintenance or gardening work needed on the property. He was a very hard-working man in his mid-sixties, who could frequently be heard calling from the lane outside:

"Mama, anything you want mi do today?"

Of course, mama more often than not had something that needed doing either on the house or in the grounds, which was spread over two acres. Aaron had a daughter, named Sharnett, who had recently come to stay with him from Spanish Town. This was after her mother, with whom she'd been living, advised her that the country air would help to control her unstable mental condition. This strategy seemed to had worked because she had managed to acquire an office administration job at the Goodyear Tyre Company in Springfield, near Morant Bay.

Looking back, as custodian of the last two of the young ones in their care, granny Henni and Rensford had certainly done a great job in teaching them practical skills they would never forget. Sonia had been taught how to sew really well, and she could not wait to show her mum what she could do with a spare remnant of material. Granny Henni often related to Sonia stories of her time living in Cuba when she was of a similar age to Sonia, and how her sewing skills had been enhanced by a woman named Portia who had a thriving dress making business. Sonia grew up knowing that story inside out, and in years to come it would aid in uncovering an important missing part of another family's meteoric rise to international fame in the world of haute couture. But all of that would come much later on.

And as for Patsy, who had been born the same year as her cousin, she had been taught how to cook really tasty traditional meals. Her favourite dish was the nation's ultimately popular 'Ackee and Salt-fish,' one that her grandfather had enjoyed showing her how to make just right. Following his death, Henni had continued helping both girls to be the best at what they liked doing, often repeating to them her favourite sayings; one of which was that 'life is what you make it', and the only person stopping them from achieving the best in life would be they themselves. And in the years to come they would find her words echoing throughout their lives.

In 1975, when Patsy's time had come for her to leave and join her parents in London, the two friendly cousins had promised to keep in touch. It would be another year before Sonia's parents did the same for her. However, true to her word, Patsy soon wrote to Sonia describing what it was like living in London. Red double decker buses, white snowflakes, and baked beans were just a few of the things she wrote about. Sonia's eyes had widened when reading, in another of her letters, about endless rows of street houses which Patsy said were like little factories puffing out smoke from the chimneys on their roofs. To Sonia, it seemed like a different world compared to life in Jamaica, but even so, she could not wait to see it all for herself.

One person really wishing she did not have to leave was her best friend, Dennis Bowen, whom she'd known from the age of nine when she and Patsy were attending the junior school in Morant Bay. At the time, twelve year old Dennis was attending the High School nearby with his younger brother, Troy. They would watch the two girls hurry pass them on their way going to school. Some mornings they all shared the same taxi, and when other kids picked on Sonia for her small size, Dennis would tell them to leave her alone. He always stuck up for his little friend, who he jokingly nicknamed, 'miss wire waist.'

Well, the years went by and through all the ups and downs of everyday life, Dennis and Sonia remained the best of friends. He matured into a tall and handsome nineteen year old, who was currently enrolled on an apprenticeship at the same tyre factory that Aaron's daughter, Sharnett, worked. And as for Sonia, she was a blossoming 16 year old, whose beauty he could see shining through more and more each day.

Something had gradually dawned on Dennis, one month prior to her departure. It was during their attendance at the annual Caribbean Festival of Arts, which was taking place that year at Prospect Beach, near Lyssons. As they were enjoying the various artistic attractions, and talking about the good times they'd spent together as kids growing up in the same neighbourhood, Dennis there and then realized that Sonia was the only girl he loved. And later on, as the sun was beginning its evening descent amidst a bright red sky, a song that depicted his feelings at that time could be heard playing on one of the festival sound systems nearby. It was called **(1) "It's You I Love" (Techniques).**

Dennis did not want her to go, but knew she had no choice, and so he'd opened up his heart that day, asking her not to forget him when she got to England. She had reassured him by looking into his eyes, promising to return one day as soon as she could afford the fare. No matter what happened, she had told him, he was her boy for life and there would be no other. He was happy to hear her speak those words and had held her close all the way home on the bus back to the village, as he pondered what his life was going to be like without having her around.

Soon, the day before her departure had come and granny Henni was talking to Sonia as she helped her pack her suitcase. She received a big hug from her granddaughter, thanking her for everything, including teaching her how to make her own clothes. Her gran smiled and told her that no matter what happened, she would always be there for her. And after saying that, granny Henni went to her bedroom for something she wanted Sonia to have. She returned with a small wooden chest, which Sonia recognised as coming from off her dressing table. It contained her granny's special things, like photos, necklaces, and her marriage certificate etc. She sat down next to Sonia and opened the box, taking out an open, solid silver, ethnic bangle of African origin.

"This is for you my dear," said her granny, "Something for you to remember me by."

"Are you sure grandma?" Sonia asked.

Henni replied that she was very sure. It had been given to her by her grandmother, and so it felt right to pass it on to the last grandchild who she'd been taking care of. Sonia thought about it deeply for a moment and then hugged her grandmother again promising to always wear it and think of her.

As well as having flattened sides, there were some curious markings on the outside that Sonia inquired about, but granny Henni had long forgotten what her own grandmother had explained to her so many years before. The only thing she did remember was that originally there was a set of two bangles belonging to an African princess who was kidnapped and sold into slavery. And even though the two pieces had been separated, the story went that one day they would be reunited. Sonia was grateful for receiving such a fantastic family heirloom.

As she remembered what was coming up the next day, Sonia was looking a little worried and confided to her grandmother how both apprehensive and excited she was about going to England and not knowing if she would actually like it there.

"Don't worry your little head, girl," granny Henni reassured her, "Life is what *you* make it, and don't ever forget that!"

"I won't, grandma," was Sonia's determined reply, "I definitely won't."

It was discussions like that with her grandmother which really made Sonia become the kind of person she developed into. Their conversations sometimes touched on the subject of boys, and her granny did not shy away from telling her about the facts of life. Sonia remembered her reading passages of scripture, from her large King James family Bible, each night before retiring. Miriam would sometimes recall fond memories of a preacher man in the 1930's, who was married to her brother in law's aunt. He'd taught them and many other villagers wonderful things from the Bible, which she and Rensford had passed on to all their children. And there was one thing they'd made sure all of their children and grandchildren learned; namely, that the proper place to have children is when you are married. Sonia was in no doubt her granny was right as she saw plenty evidence in the village of young girls struggling to cope with babies and no husband around. No, she thought to herself, she would not let that happen to her.

Later that afternoon, there was a knock at the door and outside was Dennis, who had come straight from work to be with her for the last evening. They let him in and granny offered him a cool drink from the fridge. She had a soft spot for her granddaughter's special friend and she asked them if they were going to keep in touch. They both smiled as they said yes at the same time.

"Well, don't mind me if you have things to talk about," granny told them, "I'll be out in the kitchen."

"Ok, granny," Sonia replied, with a bright smile.

They spent a while out on the front veranda listening on the radio to the popular DJ, Don Topping, who called himself 'The Caricom's El Numero Uno.' His upbeat style of broadcasting and his variety of music, catered to their age group, which they had always enjoyed tuning in to. They had certainly experienced some good times, while playing it cool, together over the years. And just as they were talking about this, the song **(2) "Play It Cool" (Alton Ellis)** came on over the radio.

Suddenly, spoiling the moment, there could be heard in the lane, someone calling out to Dennis. It was Aaron's daughter, Sharnett, who Sonia had only seen a few times passing by since her arrival from Spanish Town. The pretty, dark skinned girl, who was about the same age as Dennis, had recognized him on the veranda and seemed intent on speaking with him about something. So he got up and went over by the gate to see what she wanted. Sonia could discern that it could not be anything serious, as they both seemed to be smiling and laughing. When Sharnett eventually walked away, Sonia caught her looking back to catch a glimpse of Dennis just as he had turned around.

Dennis explained that she had recently commenced

working in the office of the factory. Sonia could sense a bit of jealousy creeping in, but dismissed it when he told her that Sharnett only wanted to know if he would be attending the company barbecue the following weekend, as she hadn't seen his name on the list of all who would be coming. His reply to her had been that, with Sonia not being around, he would be giving it a miss.

When Sonia inquired what the laughter had been about, he explained that Sharnett had made a joke about some dodgy sausages, apparently at the last company barbecue, that she'd heard had made some people ill. So, by him not going, it might actually save his life. Sonia saw the funny side too, and started to laugh herself. However, alarm bells of jealousy had started ringing in her head, which she desperately wanted to silence.

Following that interruption, as they continued listening to the radio and enjoying each others company, Sonia showed Dennis the gift she had received from her grandmother. As well as reminding her of her granny, she told him that it would always remind her of that final evening spent with him before she went to England.

Later, after a hard day's work, Dennis' brother, Troy, stopped by to say goodbye to Sonia. He had been working with their father, Derek, in the village on a house building project. As a skilled builder, Derek was teaching his youngest son all the tricks of the trade on being a good mason. Dennis had not been keen on a career in construction, which was why his father had pulled a few strings to get him the apprenticeship at the Goodyear Tyre Company.

After sunset, an hour or two later, they all took a stroll along the beach, which was just two hundred yards behind granny's house. It was a beautiful, warm January night with a full moon that seemed so close you could almost reach out and touch it. The waves gently rolled onto the pebbled beach where some other people were enjoying the evening too. Sonia was really enjoying a wonderful last night in Jamaica as they walked and joked around. At one point there could be heard a very poignant song, reflecting the love they both felt for each other, booming from a neighbour's sound system. It was **(3) "The Real Thing" (Bitty Mclean),** and when Dennis started to sing along with the chorus, Sonia remarked at what a really good singing voice he had. It certainly wasn't the first time he'd heard that because she, along with many others, had told him the same thing after hearing him sing at various times in the past. He'd always dismissed such comments, but that evening as they all walked back, Dennis told them he was actually thinking of quitting his apprenticeship with the tyre company and joining two of his friends in a band in Kingston. Sonia encouraged him to go for it because, as he was such a good singer, she was sure he would be a success. Her comments made him smile and he said he'd write to let her know his decision. His brother was very encouraging too, but wondered what their father would think as he had tried very hard to help him get the apprenticeship with Goodyear. Dennis told him not to worry about their father, they would cross that bridge when it comes.

When they arrived back at the house, Dennis gave Sonia a big hug before saying goodnight until the next day, when he would be returning to accompany her in the taxi to the airport; having already prearranged the day off from his work. Troy explained that, due to having a tight deadline with the building work with his father, he would be unable to return with his brother. However, he wished her a safe journey and all the very best for when she got to England. They left her standing on the veranda as they opened the gate and turned to walk down the lane. Troy didn't notice a tear rolling down his brother's face and he was too far from Sonia to notice one rolling down hers too.

## CHAPTER 2
### ENGLAND CALLING

It was a very rainy day in Kingston as the aeroplane prepared for its take off at 5pm. Sonia took a long last look at her beautiful island and as she peered out of the window, far in the distance on the lush green hills above the capital, she could make out a number of homes dotted about. She imagined how life for those people would be going on much the same as usual, but what about her she wondered, what kind of life laid ahead for her in England? As the plane started taxiing, she glanced down at the silver bangle and thought about her wonderful grandmother. Not one who liked waving goodbye at airports, her granny had decided against the trip to Kingston that afternoon, choosing instead to say her farewell on the front veranda as they had waited for the taxi to turn up. The plane's engines roared and, as it tore down the runway, Sonia's thoughts turned to Dennis and how he had looked so sad, waving goodbye before she had disappeared from his view into the departure lounge earlier on. Then, as the jet soared up above the rain clouds into the sunny clear blue skies, a heavy heart was what she was feeling, but in that same heart she knew one day they would be together again.

After a nine hour flight, the Air Jamaica DC-10 touched down safely on the runway amidst a cold and grey morning in London. Sonia was met in the arrivals hall of Heathrow by her parents who were beaming with delight to be reunited, after eight years, with their only daughter. Even though she had seen her mum when she had flown out to attend her father's funeral, at long last they were all together again for good. And someone else was also there to meet her too, a little person who her mother had wrote to her about. It was her new baby brother, who had been born just six months earlier. They had named him Lukie, and he looked really snug and warm in his white baby shawl and woollen bobble hat. There were a whole lot of hugs and kisses before they all walked out of the main doors towards the car park. Sonia's father, Garbert, had passed his driving test recently, and his first car was a dark green Ford Cortina MK 3. His job at the St Maria's flour mills in Bristol was a big improvement from the occupation he left in Jamaica. Back there, he had worked as part of a team of anti-malaria sprayers on a large sugar estate, called Belvedere. He remembered the long hours working in the tropical heat for the very little pay that he used to receive. How glad he had been when his brother in law, George, sent him £20 to go towards his fare on a voyage to Southampton. He was really keen to see for himself what England, the head of the commonwealth, was really like. And after only one year of working at the flour mills, he had saved up enough, both to pay back George and to send for his wife. However, Sonia had to remain in the care of her grandparents; just for one year was the original plan. But due to various financial problems, their reuniting had to wait a whole eight years. Ever since he was growing up in Jamaica, if there was one thing that Garbert really hated, it was the thought of being a poor man, and he felt sure that his job at the flour mills would be his key to getting ahead in life. He really had a good feeling about it.

Well, it was a very pleasant drive and on the way to Bristol, Sonia was struck by the variety of new sights and smells bombarding her senses. Everything was so different here, just like her cousin Patsy had described in her letters. From that first journey, Sonia realized that nothing was going to be the same again for her.

# CHAPTER 3
## THE GROVANS

Back in Jamaica, Dennis had not been very happy with the job he was being trained for at Goodyear; a singing career was what he really wanted. So, after talking it over with his father, who was none too pleased with his decision, he packed his bags and moved to Kingston with his friends, Johnny Sinclair and Norman Taylor. Johnny's grandfather, Maurice Sinclair, along with some friends had been the force behind what eventually became 'Happitone Music' in Jamaica in the 1950s.

So, it was no surprise that Johnny and his good friend, Norman, wanted to pursue a career in music. However, despite his father's musical legacy, Johnny did not want to enlist any help from him due to the way his mother had been mistreated by him when he was a youngster. Johnny was determined to make it without his assistance.

Meanwhile, before Dennis had left for Kingston, his father had given him his blessing, telling him to do whatever his heart moved him to do and that he would not stand in his way; Dennis really appreciated his father for saying that.

Johnny and Norman had formed a band, going by the name 'The Grovans,' and Dennis had accepted their invitation to join them. Their harmonies were perfect, and Dennis was chosen as lead vocalist due to his tremendous range. It was obvious to everyone who heard them that they were headed for the top, and on many occasions people would gather around them, giving cheers as they practised on Fort Clarence Beach, which was not too far from where they lived in the Portmore district, and this made them feel real good.

Due to their popularity on the local scene, it was not surprising that they were spotted one evening at the Globe Theatre by Errol Thompson, an executive for the Joe Gibbs recording studio. Known as the 'Mighty Two,' Joe Gibbs and Errol Thompson had produced massive hits for local artists, and were always on the lookout for fresh new talent. The Globe Theatre, on Orange Street, was a very popular local venue where new talent was showcased once a month. Performers paid just J$25.00 for a five minute slot on the exciting Friday evening special called, 'Hit or Miss.' The audience would decide by their applause who the 'Hit' artists were on the night, and the winners had a chance to get a record produced by one of the numerous recording studios in Kingston.

On that particular summer evening in August 1976, 'The Grovans' performed a love song entitled **(4) "Miss Wire Waist" (Carl Malcolm)** which Dennis had written depicting his love for Sonia. He had certainly surprised himself with song writing skills which he never realized he possessed. Well, they brought the house down with rapturous applause, winning the night's contest and an invitation by Errol Thompson to discuss not just a one off record but a recording contract. The lads were on cloud nine and agreed to meet the next day at the company's studio on Maxfield Avenue.

The contract was nothing really fantastic, with open clauses for all parties to opt out without penalties. And even though royalties were heavily weighed on the company's side, the lads were glad for their big break into show business. They could each now afford to rent their own one bedroom apartments in Mona Heights, and the good life was just beginning.

During that time, Dennis had written several letters to Sonia, telling her all about his musical success with the band and hoping she would be coming back soon for a visit. Initially she had replied quickly to all his letters, praising him for his success with the band. However, after around ten months or so, something occurred that started those alarm bells of jealousy ringing again in her head, causing her to doubt his love for her. It all began one evening when Sonia rang the phone number to his apartment, and the voice of a young woman answered, asking her what she wanted.

"I'm sorry," replied Sonia, thinking that she must have misdialled, "I wanted to speak with Dennis Bowen."

"What you want fi speak with my Dennis fa?" the woman flared, "You can't find no other man except fi tek mine?"

Following that, she'd just slammed down the phone on Sonia...

Sonia, certain that she had not dialled the wrong number, did not know what to make of the woman's outburst. Who could she be?...And what was she doing in Dennis' apartment?...Had he really got another girl, after all the years they'd known each other?...And if that was true, did he think he could keep it secret from her?...

Her head was sure in a muddle, and she knew the best way to resolve the situation would be to confront him about it as soon as she could get to talk with him directly.

What she did not know was that the woman was the same person she had seen speaking with Dennis on her final day in Jamaica. Yes, it was Sharnett, who had become a deranged fan of 'The Grovans,' and of Dennis in particular. She had secretly been obsessed with him, while he was working at the factory, and when he left she had gone out of her mind. Very soon after that she had quit her job in order to follow Dennis and the band wherever they went.

That particular day, she had broken her way into Dennis' apartment, awaiting his arrival home. She was hoping to get him to accept her as his only girlfriend. To her dismay, however, when he got home and confronted her, the police were quickly summoned. In a short time they arrived with their sirens blaring, disturbing the peace of the uptown neighbourhood, and apprehended the crazy stalker as she kicked and screamed out to Dennis to save her. All she could think was that, if it was not for Sonia, he could be all hers; she was just one girl too late, like the song **(5) "One Girl Too Late" (Anthony 'Pure Silk' Brightly & Winsome)** says.

Dennis looked at her with pity, wondering just what was going on in her mind, and also thinking what he could do to help her. Later, when the police asked if he would be pressing charges, he told them he'd rather see to it that she got proper medical treatment for her condition, which he was sure her parents would appreciate.

When Sonia called again later that evening, she found his story, about Sharnett the stalker, a little hard to believe. Dennis realised he had to convince her, and the words of the song **(6) "Baby Please" (Peter Hunnigale)** came to his mind, which he sang to her down the phone. Well, it all sounded quite implausible, and even though she finally accepted it, there remained a lingering doubt. Was she really beginning to turn her back on Dennis, whom she'd promised would be her boy for life?...

Well, during the following year 'The Grovans' performed their hits at open air concerts all over the island and were loved everywhere they went. Many girls would scream when they saw Dennis, who was by far the best looking of the trio, as well as being the lead singer. His autographs were in constant demand and, not to mention, his hugs too. In fact he found himself having to fight them off at many venues. But despite his popularity, he felt that his heart was already taken and no other girl could take Sonia's place.

However, things got worse in Sonia's mind, a few weeks later, when she read an article about the band's success in the Jamaica Gleaner newspaper. It made a big splash about their being very popular with the girls, who screamed out for them at concerts, and especially for Dennis. She began thinking to herself whether he could really be trusted to stay clear from their advances, while she was nearly five thousand miles away in England. She knew she should have known him better than that, but she just could not help thinking negatively about it.

Deep in her heart, Sonia knew she still loved Dennis, but the increasing sound of the bells of jealousy were beginning to make her to turn her back on him. The song **(7) "Jealousy" (T.T. Ross)** sums up how she was feeling at that time.

So, Dennis, despite being very busy touring with the band, kept writing to her whenever he could. And Sonia, though very much wanting to be certain of his love for her, found herself engrossed with a new two year college course she had enrolled in, and so his letters hardly got answered. Even so, he kept writing to her, whether or not he got a reply. All he wished was for her to drop him a line to say she was doing fine.

She was actually very busy studying fashion design, to enhance the skills in dressmaking that her granny had instilled in her. Sonia did not mean to start turning her back on Dennis, the one person she had only ever loved, but in her head there were unresolved issues of jealousy which she had to deal with. She was sure it could all be sorted in time, but there were also many distractions in her new life in England...

One particular distraction was a young man called Leon, who she met at a house party shortly after her arrival. Her mother had arranged the party to celebrate the family's reunion, and Leon was invited with his mother, who was called Queenie. She was Sandra's best friend, whose husband was living in Toronto following his permanent residence status which had been granted three months earlier. Leon was their only son, and they all planned to be relocating to Canada as soon as he completed college, which would take about 18 months.

At the party, Leon soon instigated a friendship with Sonia from the time he first saw her. He was struck by her beauty, her smile, and easygoing nature.

Dennis had no idea of what was going on and so all he could imagine was that Sonia had begun to forget him and the beautiful feelings they had shared. He felt that, if he just kept writing to her, she would be bound to see how much he still cared and hopefully not forget what they had. During that upsetting time, Dennis wrote his most famous hit song for the band called, **(8) "Money In My Pocket" (Dennis Brown)** with one poignant line that describes how he cannot believe it when she says that she is coming, since she departed from him on a rainy day.

After a year of recording top hits, 'The Grovans'

decided to part company with 'The Mighty Two' in September 1977, and subsequently signed up with Clement Dodd's Studio One record label. By then they had a growing fan base in North America, and in 1979 their management team arranged for them to perform in a few clubs and small venues in New York and Chicago. Then came one offer they could not refuse, which was to tour with Bob Marley and the Wailers in the UK, in January 1980.

By that time, Dennis and Sonia's lives were moving in completely different directions. He was in a top reggae band preparing for a UK tour with Bob Marley, and she was too busy with her life in England to even find time to call or drop him a line. It seemed that whatever love they once had for each other was lost in the fog of life and would forever stay that way.

# CHAPTER 4
## BACK A YARD

Late in the month of December 1979, just a few weeks before leaving Jamaica for the UK tour, Dennis took a trip up country to say farewell to his folks. During the taxi ride from Kingston, which took about an hour to reach Grovan Pen, the driver played a cassette tape featuring one particular song that really put Dennis in the mood for the journey. It was called **(9) "Country Living" (Sandra Cross).**

Finally, after the taxi drove Dennis past some familiar sights in the village, it stopped outside of a very familiar three bedroomed wood panelled bungalow. As he approached the gate, Dennis was glad when he saw his old man; busy in the yard using a long bamboo pole to cut down some ripe breadfruits from a fully laden tree. A sharp knife attached to the end of the bamboo made it easy work. When he turned and saw his eldest son, Derek was very pleased, and the two of them had a big hug under the breadfruit tree. Troy came home later that afternoon, after working hard rebuilding a new wall for a local family in the village. His father had taught him well, and his services were always in demand. They all spent the rest of the evening catching up on old times and playing dominoes with a few of Derek's local friends. All of this was accompanied by copious bottles of Red Stripe beer.

During the few days spent with his family, Dennis made a visit to the covered market in Morant Bay, as he needed to buy some personal items in preparation for the tour. Whilst there, he heard the voice of an old lady bartering with another woman over the price of some cotton briefs she had on display. It was a voice he knew well, and when she turned and saw him she smiled and gave him a warm embrace. Yes, it was Sonia's granny Henni, still doing business at her ripe old age, with the stall which she had first started over forty years before. She was really happy to see him and inquired how he was doing. Dennis was glad to see her too and after telling her about his upcoming tour, she asked if he was going to see Sonia when he got to England. He explained to her that they had not actually been in touch for quite a while, and was not really sure if he would even have the time to look her up. She was sorry to hear him say that, but then held his hands and squeezed them tight, telling him not to give up on Sonia, because she always believed that the two of them were made for each other. As they parted, Dennis thought about what she had said and he had to admit that she was right. It was obvious to him why he hadn't found himself interested in any other girls who had come his way. Sonia was his one love who had never ever departed from his heart, and so he was determined to get in touch with her and be prepared to accept whatever he may find.

On the evening before he was due to return to Kingston, Derek arranged a farewell party for his son. The house was rocking with music from a sound system set up by Troy and some friends. When they played **(10) "I'm Still Waiting" (Delroy Wilson)**, Dennis thought about Sonia and how he was prepared to wait patiently for her, because he was sure granny Henni was right with what she said about the two of them. He wished Sonia could have been there to enjoy the evening with him and all his family and friends. The smell of jerk chicken was more intoxicating than the rum and coke.

Everyone was wishing Dennis all the best for the UK tour, including his mother, Jasmine, who had travelled across from Port Antonio especially to see her big son. She and her husband had not been living together for a number of years. They had gradually grown apart from each other ever since he had begun working away from home doing farm work in Panama. That began in the late 60's, and Jasmine found with him being away for such long periods that she had to be the one making all the decisions around the home. Eventually it got to the point where she felt she just did not need him around.

Although Derek always sent money over for her, as an independent woman she wanted to make her own money; which was the reason why she got a job at the post office in Port Antonio. She took their boys, who at the time were just ten and nine years old respectively, to live with her in Portland at her mother's place. Her name was Grace, and she was a great help in those times, while Derek continued living in the family home in Grovan Pen. However, as the years had progressed and he had finished working away, the boys stayed with him every now and then, and when Jasmine had an opportunity to travel to the States for work, they moved back in with him full time.

Jasmine had remained in the States, working as a nanny for a wealthy family, for almost five years with the occasional trip back home to see her boys and their father. She had always retained a special spot in her heart for Derek and he always knew it too. Despite this, however, the two of them never really got round to talking things over.

Eventually, with the help of her employers, she acquired her green card for American Citizenship. Although it was quite an achievement, in fact something highly sought after by many, after about a year or so she got really homesick and subsequently decided that she had actually had enough of America and wanted to return home to Jamaica for good.

Derek was not one to show his feelings but he did write her a letter once, when she was in the states, that contained the words of a song which summed up how he was feeling. He really felt sorry over their separation, and did not want to keep his feelings locked up inside forever. The words he penned were from **(11) "Crying Over You" (Ken Boothe).** Jasmine had received the letter but had not given a reply, though deep down she felt that she was falling back in love with him for the second time. Hiding her true feelings she felt like the song, **(12) "Hurting On The Inside" (Sammy Levi)** was written just for her. However, her independent spirit made her be like a stranger to her heart and keep it all locked up inside. Well, that was all in the past now and at least they had two lovely sons to be proud of despite everything else.

Now, also at the party was Jasmine's mother, Grace, who could read her daughter and son in law like a book. She could see they both had feelings for each other even after all those years of living apart. Grace saw them talking in the kitchen and approached offering them some words of wisdom. Among the things she said was that life is a game and people do make mistakes along the way, but they needed to remember that it's all in the game. Just then Troy put the ideal song on the turntable called **(13) "All In The Game" (One Blood).** It was the turning point they had both longed for and Derek looked Jasmine in her eyes and asked for a dance which she accepted, melting into his arms. Dennis and Troy were amazed at what they were seeing and so were everyone else that night. So thanks to her mother's intervention, Jasmine and her husband were back together again.

# CHAPTER 5
## GAMES PEOPLE PLAY

In the meantime, over in England back in 1978, Sonia had kept putting Leon off whenever he would invite her out, because she simply could not forget the promise she had made to Dennis, despite lingering feelings of jealousy. She had explained to Leon about her deep feelings for Dennis, but he was not one to be put off something once he had set his sights on it. He really liked Sonia and so, in his attempts at wooing her, he would send flowers or chocolates and at other times he wrote her poems.

One of his most heartfelt poems extolled his admiration for her from the very first time he had blessed his eyes on her, when he pictured her to be his bride. He must have been listening to a song called **(14) "I Admire You" (Roland & Carolyn)** because those sentiments are conveyed in the lyrics. His tactics eventually worked, and Sonia agreed to go with him to a local sports centre one Saturday evening where he'd be playing basketball with some friends. It was a great evening and after the game they all went for a pizza down on the Centre in a restaurant near the Hippodrome. They repeated this kind of weekend fun for a few more times, but despite having such good times with Leon, Sonia was in two minds. It was so hard and confusing for her to decide what to do about the two men in her life.

Eventually, after around six months, she told Leon he would have to give her time to think about whether or not she'd be going out with him again. This came as a shock to Leon who thought he'd had her in the palm of his hands. And then after much soul searching, she made her decision which was to be true to her first love and, sadly, Leon had to accept the fact that he had lost her. Now, even though she had made that decision, she still found herself too busy to find time to write or call Dennis and clear up things that were still troubling her. This was all due to the fact she was putting all her concentration into her college course, and later that year in October 1978, she successfully completed it.

Following all of that, Sonia had moved to London to work for 'Barnaby's, a designer-wear boutique chain, who had accepted her as their junior fashion designer in January 1979. Her family supported her decision to move to London to further her career, and her cousin Patsy invited her to share her bedroom in her family home in Leytonstone, east London. Patsy's dad, George, was Sandra's older brother who together with his wife, Hazel, were only too pleased to have their niece stay with them in London. Patsy was their only child and so Sonia would be great company for her since they were also good friends anyway.

Now, as for Leon, he couldn't really get Sonia out of his mind so easily after her decision to finish with him, and so he could be heard playing a particular record over and over in his bedroom which summed up his feelings about Sonia. The song was **(15) "Never Gonna Give You Up" (Jean Adebambo).** He looked for any excuse to be near her, and an opportunity arose just a short time after her move to London. He overheard Sandra and his mother planning a visit to see her, and promptly offered to drive them down as Garbert said he could not do it due work commitments at the flour mills. Despite what Sonia had said, he just wanted to see her again and maybe change her mind.

When they were there in London, Leon's mother, was unashamedly rooting for her son when she asked Sonia if she did not want a boyfriend, even though she was well aware of Dennis over in Jamaica. So Sonia had her job cut out fending off both mother and son on that occasion. It was a nice weekend spent with the family, and Sonia really enjoyed being with her mum. When it was time to leave, Leon had whispered something in Sonia's ear about wishing she would give him another chance to prove how much he cared about her. But she gave him a smile and a hug telling him that despite his being a sweet guy she was not going to change her mind. He told her that he hoped they could still be friends.

"Don't worry Leon," she reassured him, as he took took the bags to the car, "you'll always be a good friend to me."

He liked that and thought to himself that being good friend to Sonia was better than being nothing at all.

After Sandra had finished saying her goodbyes to her brother and his wife, she gave Sonia and Patsy one final big squeeze and then both she and Queenie got into Leon's car and made their way back to Bristol along the M4 motorway.

Now, Sonia was not the only one to have trouble with people playing games with her. Her cousin Patsy had her own troubles too...

Patsy had done very well in her chosen career as a Chef, after being taught to cook so well in Jamaica by her grandparents. After two years of study, at a college in the east of London, she had achieved her qualifications in professional cookery and was fortunate to get a job straight away with the Intercontinental Park Lane hotel as a Chef De Partie. It was a great job that she enjoyed doing, and in time there would be opportunities to advance to higher positions in the company.

While at college she had become friendly with a young man called Delroy, who was doing a course on Business Studies. They talked together a few times during lunch but nothing really got off the ground. Patsy really liked him, but sometimes when they met outside of college, he seemed to be playing games and ignoring her. Once, when she saw him with his mother at a bus stop in Knightsbridge, he didn't even acknowledge her when she said hello. This had really upset her and when she confronted him about it, the following week at college, he acted as if he couldn't remember what he had done. To make it up to her he invited her to the cinema to watch 'Star Wars,' but she told him that she'd prefer to see 'Annie Hall.' So it was that their first official date was to watch the Woody Allen movie in the heart of the West End at the Empire, Leicester Square cinema. But after that great night out things did not improve with their relationship, with Delroy failing to take Patsy's feelings about him seriously. She asked him pointedly one day what he would do with her heart if she gave it to him. Maybe it was to do with him being a year younger than her, but whatever the reason, to Patsy it seemed like her feelings for him were on a one way street and he would tear her heart apart if she allowed him. Patsy wondered to herself what would be the point of starting something you can't continue. It was as if she was reading the words of a song called **(16) "If I Gave My Heart To You" (John Mclean).**

She and Sonia spent many an evening discussing her on and off relationship with Delroy. Sometimes the conversation drifted onto Dennis, who Sonia had been talking about constantly when she first came over to England. But Sonia would say, even though she knew Dennis was the only guy she wanted, she really was too busy to keep in touch; what with first, her college course, and then her demanding job. Deep down she did feel guilty about this and she promised herself that she really must find out how he was doing.

## CHAPTER 6
### FORGET ME NOT

After spending less than a year living with her cousin's family, Sonia decided to move into her own two bed rented apartment on the Chelsea embankment, which she could easily afford. It was January 1980 and she was thrilled when given the assistant designer's role for a company on Oxford Street called Havandora Fashion House. They were a top international fashion empire with branches in Miami, New York, and Paris. Sonia was very proud to be working for such a prestigious company.

Life certainly was good for the young twenty year

old and she never forgot that it was all due to her granny Henni's brilliant skills instilled in her so many years before.

On a cold evening, early in that first month of the year, as she was sitting in her warm lounge reminiscing, Sonia received an unusually late phone call from her mother in Bristol. From the way she spoke her name, Sonia knew something was wrong. Her mother was in tears, informing her that granny Henni had passed away in Jamaica. They all knew she couldn't live on forever, after all she was nearly ninety five, but no one could bear the thought of it happening. Sonia was deeply saddened by the news, especially as she had been meaning to give both Dennis and her grandmother a call, but due to work schedules she had kept putting it off. And now it was too late. She spent the rest of that evening searching for the silver bangle that she had promised to always wear, but which had long been misplaced. Eventually, it was found at the bottom of a drawer full of clutter.

"Oh, granny," she cried to herself. "How could I have forgotten?"

She remembered the words of a song all about taking time to say the important things to the ones you love while they are still living, and realized it was so true. The song was **(17) "In The Living Years" (Stevie Face).**

Both young women were allowed some time off from their workplaces for compassionate leave, and they decided to return to Jamaica for the funeral along with other members of the family. The flight was due to leave on January 14th, which coincidentally happened to be the same day that Dennis and his band mates were due to arrive in the UK to begin their tour.

What would be the chances of their paths crossing that day?...

Patsy's father drove the London crew to Heathrow that Sunday morning in time for the 12pm departure. He was a very humorous man; the eldest of Henni's children who, along with his wife and daughter, was also booked on the Air Jamaica flight. Sandra and four year old Lukie met them all in the check-in area of Heathrow's Terminal Three, after arriving there by coach. Garbert would have driven them there, but he was unable to get the time off from his work at the flour mills. Anyway, with there being talk of redundancies and the imminent closure of the depot, he wanted to stick around just in case of any important developments. It was his first job since arriving in Britain in 1965, and with a fifteen year redundancy package, he would, as he repeatedly stated, "never be a poor man again." Well, he'd have to wait to see what happened.

At the airport, everyone was glad to see each other, and once checked in they made their way into the departure lounge. All were happy to be going to Jamaica but, at the same time, sad for the reason for their visit. As they waited and talked, Sandra remembered that Dennis had phoned the house asking for Sonia the day before, and she had given him her apartment phone number. The last time Dennis had spoken to Sonia was when she was living in Bristol with her family, which was about three years before. Sandra had been very pleased to hear from him and had explained that Sonia had moved to London and living in her own apartment, just like him. Before ending the call, she had informed him about the death of granny Henni and the plans she and Sonia were making to come out for the funeral with a few other relatives on a flight leaving on the 14th of January. He was very sorry to hear that sad news, especially as he had only been speaking with granny Henni in the market a little while back.

"Did he call you, Sonia?" Sandra inquired.

"Yes, we had a good talk," replied Sonia. "he was really upset about granny."

"I thought you told me you were too busy for him, Sonia," her mother questioned.

"I am, mum," was her reply, "but Dennis is just my old friend; a friend who I've never given up on despite everything."

"I understand his band are touring with Bob Marley over here soon," Sandra continued, "will you go to one of their concerts?"

"Possibly," she replied to her mum, "they'll actually be at the London Lyceum for two nights to close their tour in February. Hey guys, when we get back shall I get us all tickets for the show?"

They all agreed that it would be a great night out, and then Patsy smiled at her cousin and asked if she wasn't a little bit interested to see her old friend again. Sonia repeated to her that she and Dennis were just old friends who had lost touch and nothing more.

"Ok, Ok," replied Patsy, "just remember to invite me to the wedding."

"You mean after you and Delroy's wedding first don't you?" Sonia responded, jokingly.

This started them all laughing, after which they heard the announcement for their flight to begin boarding on gate number 5.

What Sonia had not disclosed to them was how Dennis had poured out his feelings to her. He had emotionally expressed how he had written to her several times, eager to know how she was getting on over there, with no response. Even her home number had been changed, due to her move to London, without her notifying him. However, despite everything, when all was said and done, he told her he would be prepared to take the blame for loving her too much, and that he just wanted to know if the love they had was still there. It was just like he was singing the song **(18) "Push Come To Shove" (Freddie Mcgregor).** As Dennis had been speaking, Sonia had begun remembering how she used to feel so many years before, and the promise she had made to return and be with him someday. Any lingering thoughts of jealousy had disappeared instantly, and she had told him that she was sorry to have made him blue, waiting so long without a word from her. As they had continued talking, she had expressed how the fault was all hers, she had just been a little mixed up inside. She was almost singing the song **(19) "I'm So Sorry" (Carroll Thompson)** and had ended saying that as soon as she got back from the funeral they should catch up when he had some free time off after the tour. He had agreed and said he couldn't wait to see her again. There were really big smiles on both their faces when the call ended.

If they could have met at Heathrow that morning, it would have been really great, but the paths of Dennis and Sonia did not cross there, and the Air Jamaica jet took to the skies for the nine hour transatlantic flight.

## CHAPTER 7
### HELLO STRANGER

It was a very hot Sunday afternoon in Kingston when the jet touched down at Kingston's Norman Manley International airport, and all on board gave a big cheer and loud claps, praising the Lord and the crew for a safe journey and landing. Lukie asked if they were actually in Jamaica now, after being told by his mum they were not there yet all through the flight.

She was glad to inform him finally, "Yes, Lukie, we are in Jamaica now."

His eyes lit up with all the excitement a four year old could muster and exclaimed, "Yippee, I can't wait to see it."

He made all those around him smile.

A short time later when they had all cleared through immigration and customs, after collecting their luggage from the baggage hall, they exited the main doors of the airport into the bright hot sunshine. Immediately they were barraged by numerous taxi and minibus drivers vying for trade. Their services were not required, however, because Sandra had arranged with her cousin, who lived in Kingston, to pick them up. Her name was Ruby, and she was there with friendly minibus driver Douglas Brown, a.k.a Duggy Fresh, to collect her family.

When she saw them, she told the driver, "See them deh!"

And then she ran over as she shouted out to her cousin, "Sandra, what happen cuz?"

"Hey Ruby, we're fine. It's been such a long time, and you're looking good," Sandra replied, with a beaming smile. "thanks for meeting us."

It had been many years since they had seen each other, so the greetings and laughter went on for quite a while. The only unfamiliar face was Lukie, who was introduced to her as the others assisted Duggy Fresh to pack all the luggage into the minibus.

Suddenly, as they all started getting into the vehicle, Sonia heard a very familiar voice call out from behind her, "Hey, Miss wire waist," Yes, it was none other than Dennis!

Sonia turned and saw Dennis approaching with arms outstretched to wrap around her. It seemed like a mighty long time as they embraced, oblivious to the others looking on from the mini bus. The lyrics of the song **(20) "Hello Stranger" (Brown Sugar)** was ideal for that moment.

Sonia's head was in a spin, "But what about your UK tour?" she asked, looking puzzled.

Dennis had a big smile on his face, and to Sonia he seemed even more handsome than when she last saw him four years before.

"Why don't you ride with me in my car," he suggested. "and I'll explain everything."

She agreed and, after introducing him to everyone, she told her family they'd be following behind on the way up to the family home. Her mother and Patsy just laughed among themselves, knowing that Sonia definitely had not told them the full story about her and Dennis.

Duggy Fresh drove the minibus out of the airport parking area and headed for the main road out, which seemed to be built in the middle of the sea. It was the Palisades Road, with the sea on one side and Kingston harbour on the other. Dennis and Sonia were following behind in a white Toyota Corolla which Dennis had bought recently in Kingston. The windows were wound down, they had their dark shades on, the sunroof was open and, with the wind flowing through Sonia's hair, the perfect song playing on the radio was **(21) "Breezin" (Tradition)**.

Dennis explained that he had changed his flight from Saturday to Tuesday, as the tour did not kick off until the following Friday. He had done this because, after speaking to her on the phone, he just wanted to see her as soon as he could and give her a big surprise. Sonia smiled and told him it was the best surprise she could ever have asked for. It was the greatest feeling being with Dennis again, and he was feeling the same way, even though it meant being together just for a day or two. Along the journey they discussed each other's careers and the amazing success they had both achieved so far. They also talked about granny Henni's death and all the great things she had done for her family.

"I see you're still wearing the silver bangle she gave you," observed Dennis.

Sonia confessed about forgetting her promise to her granny, but said that from then on she was determined it would not leave her body. To her it now symbolized Dennis being lost out of her life, but who had now returned.

When Sonia asked about his apartment in Kingston, he told her it was fine, but he was staying with his folks for the next few days before his flight. She smiled to herself, glad to know he'd be close by until he had to go.

Jamaica was sure looking good to Sonia and, as she enjoyed the ride to Grovan Pen, memories came flooding back as they passed several towns and villages along the coastal route. In Yallahs, the minibus stopped by some street vendors for Ruby who wanted to buy some akees, which she knew would be much cheaper than in Kingston. As she got out of the minibus, one of the vendors, a slim woman in her fifties, ran over to her with a basket of mangoes hoping for a sale. Ruby ignored her and went over to another younger woman who was selling akees, enquiring about her prices. She bartered with her until she was satisfied she had a good deal. At this point, the first vendor started ranting on about how it was her who came over first and was almost demanding a sale too. Ruby looked at her basket of fruits and decided to buy a few 'East Indian' mangoes just to keep the peace.

While this was going on, a Sky-Juice vendor was pushing his wagon full of a multitude of coloured syrups and crushed ice, "Sky juice, sky juice," he shouted out.

Lukie asked what a sky juice was as Ruby re-entered the minibus, and an explanation by his mum was simply not enough. He wanted to try a sky juice for himself, so Patsy said she'd get him one. She looked over to Sonia and asked her if she wanted one too.

"Yes please, strawberry," was her reply, "my first one in four years."

As Sonia sipped on the bag of juice, she thought about everything that had happened to bring them to that moment. A sound system was playing a beautiful song nearby which summed up her feelings. It was entitled, **(22) "Looking Over Love" (Kofi).**

Well, eventually they arrived in Grovan Pen, where Sandra and George were pleased to see all their siblings again. Ethel and Valerie had travelled by themselves from the United States, and from Canada, their youngest brother, Marcus, was there too with his wife, Ena. The only grandchildren attending the funeral were Sonia, Lukie, and Patsy, who were sorry their other cousins weren't able to make it.

Granny Henni's home was the centre point where they all gathered. Ruby had to return to Kingston as her daughter, Dominique, had a wedding coming up soon and there were still lots to arrange, but she said that she would be returning for the funeral the following week. At around 8pm she waved goodbye as Duggy Fresh pulled away sounding a beep on his horn.

Everyone spent the rest of the evening catching up with one another and remembering granny Henni and some things she used to say and do. Valerie certainly had a lot to talk about, be it her sons, her brownstone house in Brooklyn, her nursing job, or her big American car; she would go on and on, with funny anecdotes interspersed along the way. Ethel was a little more subdued, keeping her cards close to her chest. But she was proud to talk about her husband, Carlton, whom she'd left looking after their three children at their home in Miami. Her eldest girl, Blossom, was studying law at the university, which was something she was happy to tell everyone about.

Well, it was really great being together again, bringing back to their minds the times when they were just kids growing up. Marcus remarked to his wife that something smelled really nice from out in the kitchen, which reminded him of their mother's cooking.

"It's making me feel really hungry," he told her.

Patsy had been busy cooking a great evening dinner for everyone, extolling the skills of the top chef that she was. When it was ready, she put the food out in a buffet style, so they could all help themselves to what they wanted. Everyone enjoyed the wonderful meal.

Sonia and Dennis did not want the evening to end, as they knew he had to be in Kingston two days time for his flight to London. Later that evening, after the meal, Patsy joined the two love-birds outside on the back veranda relaxing on granny's comfy three piece wicker suite. In amongst the bushes in the garden, fireflies could be seen illuminating the foliage as they darted about and, as the girls slowly drank some Red Label wine, they talked about how good it was to be back home in Jamaica enjoying the beautiful warm evening. Dennis, with a bottle of Red Stripe beer in hand, asked them what was stopping them from returning. The same reply came from them both; their work. They were both so busy with their careers that returning to Jamaica was not in the equation right then. Dennis told them that no matter where he goes or what he does, he knows he will always be coming back home to his island. He then offered to take them to visit a few places before he left for London, and the girls smiled at the offer, as such an opportunity to visit other places on the island had not occurred while they were growing up with their grandparents.

Dennis told them he'd come around in the morning to take them out for the day, and it was nearly midnight when he got up to leave. He gave Sonia a peck on her cheek after a long squeeze and wished them both a good nights sleep. His parent's house, at the other side of Grovan Pen, was about a five minute drive. His mother and Troy were still up when he got home and told them about the day trip he was planning for Sonia and Patsy in the morning. It sounded like a great idea to Troy, who asked if he could tag along too as he had some free time on Monday. His brother replied that of course he could, and that it would be a great day.

"Mum, you've got to meet Sonia and her family," Dennis told his mother, "she's my number one girl, always was."

Jasmine remarked on how good it was to see him so happy, and that both she and Derek would be going over to visit Sonia and her family in a few days, as well as attending the funeral. It was also going to be good to see Ethel again, remembering how nice it had been to act as her chief bridesmaid when she married Carlton, so many moons ago.

# CHAPTER 8
## THE DAY TRIP

The next day dawned with the sun appearing brighter than ever, in the early Monday morning Caribbean skies. Outside in the yard, Dennis was awakened by the sound of his mother's roosters with their usual morning calls. Jasmine also had a number of hens running about, and Derek kept a goat and two pigs on the land too. Dennis knew he couldn't slumber that morning, and so got his brother up and the two of them prepared for the outing. The young men scrubbed up quite well, and looked very smart in their khaki shirts and lightweight cotton trousers.

They arrived at Henni's house at 8am and saw the young ladies waiting on the front veranda, looking beautiful in the hazy morning sunlight. Lukie ran out and joined them, saying he wanted to go too, but his mum shouted from inside the kitchen for him to come back in. He returned to her only after Patsy had promised to bring something back for him later.

Troy's eyes had been transfixed onto Patsy's as soon as he had seen her, and she couldn't help staring back at him too. They had very little memories of when they last saw each other, which was before Patsy had left for England about five years earlier, when she was 15 and he was 16. However, after a re-introduction by Sonia, they started talking to each other and no one could shut them up. They reminisced about the times when they all shared the taxi going to school, which was so long ago. All four of them chuckled when they thought about their innocent childhood days.

The first stop was about an hour's journey for breakfast at a popular spot on Port Antonio harbour front called "Chefs." There they enjoyed a full platter of ackee and salt-fish with callaloo and fried dumplings while overlooking the boats and yachts moored on the calm blue waters.

"Jamaica is so beautiful," remarked Patsy. "Remind me again why we left, Sonia."

"I've been asking myself that question ever since we touched down yesterday Pats," was her reply, "and if it wasn't for poor granny's death, we might not have returned for years."

"Yes, that's so true, imagine that," agreed Patsy.

Then Dennis asked them the same question he'd asked the day before, about what was stopping them from returning. And the same answer came back; it was their work.

Troy told them they could return to Jamaica, and with their skills work shouldn't be too hard to find.

"Well, you keep saying that and we may just do it," Sonia laughed, with Patsy nodding her head in agreement.

After breakfast, as they went back to the car, Dennis asked if everyone had brought their swimming gear. They all had, and so they headed back the way they'd come for their next destination, which was the Golden Shore Resort, situated in the Lyssons area of St Thomas. Dennis' band had recently played there and the manager, Mr Reid, had been so impressed with their performance that he'd invited them to return whenever they wished to enjoy the resort facilities with their friends. As they all entered the reception area, the manager recognized and greeted Dennis, who asked if they could use the beach and go for a swim. The manager not only agreed, he gave them keys to two suites for them to use as changing rooms. His kindness was really appreciated and so the girls took one room while the guys took the other.

It was a charming resort set in a secluded area, away from the hustle and bustle of everyday normal Jamaican life. After swimming in the beautiful warm sea, they all sat in the Gazebo bar and enjoyed a light refreshing non alcoholic cocktail. The resident DJ was playing a great love song that the boys imagined they were singing to the girls **(23) "Number 1 Girl" (Barry Boom)** and everyone there were just nodding their heads to the cool beat.

Patsy then remembered that she had promised to bring something back for Lukie,

"Is there a mall around here?" she asked Troy, "I want to buy something for Lukie."

"No, but there are some nice places to shop in Kingston," he replied, looking at his brother with a smile.

"Wow, are we going to Kingston today, Dennis?" Sonia asked, excitedly.

"Well, I wanted to stop by my apartment to pick up some half written lyrics for our next single that I forgot to take with me. So I don't see why we can't check out a mall at the same time," Dennis told everyone, "come on, let's roll."

So they went back to their suites to get dressed and then, after saying farewell to the manager, Dennis drove on with eager anticipation to the capital.

# CHAPTER 9
## KINGSTON TOWN

After just over an hour's drive along the south coast road, they entered the down-town area of Kingston, where on some streets could be seen people selling all kinds of wares. As they drove past Randy's Record Mart, on North Parade, there was a song booming from the sound system set up outside the premises. It was a beautiful love song extolling positive nature of the capital itself, **(24) "Kingston Town" (Lord Creator).**

"Gwaan, Dennis!" came a shout from Vincent Chin, the owner of Randy's. He recognised Dennis as they waited in traffic outside the store. Dennis smiled at him and waved as he drove on past. Vincent had long wanted 'The Grovans' to record in his Studio 17, recording centre above the store, but that had not materialized. Anyway the boys were happy with Studio 1 and everything that Clement Dodd had done for them so far.

There were many of such similar shout outs from Dennis' fans that day as they drove around. He was a well loved and very popular singer. As they continued on, they also passed by Coronation Market, which was packed with sellers of colourful fruits and vegetables and much more besides. This was the real hard working, buying and selling Jamaican life that the girls recognized. They remembered how, during school holidays, they used to help their granny on her stall in the Morant Bay Market. It was a fun part of their lives while growing up in Jamaica that they would never forget.

Dennis then took the Mountain View Road that led up to the Stoney Hill area of the capital. A few more miles and they were entering the Mona Heights district, a very smart suburb of uptown Kingston, with palm tree lined avenues and pristine homes boasting well maintained gardens. Once they had arrived at his apartment, Dennis showed them around and gave them all a cool drink. Then, having collected the lyrics, they headed off to the retail quarter. It was a very modern and metropolitan area with big buildings, shopping malls, banks and expensive homes. They stopped off at Paradise Plaza, a mall situated just a little way up past the Halfway Tree junction, where they saw many tourists having a good time in the extremely hot tropical weather. Sonia and Patsy had never been in that part of the capital, and remarked at how fantastic uptown looked compared to the downtown area of Kingston.

While Troy and Patsy went into a toy shop to try and find something for Lukie, Dennis and Sonia found themselves looking into a real classy jewellery shop window. Some beautiful diamond bracelets caused Sonia to remark how she'd love to be able to wear one some day.

"Well, it doesn't cost anything to try them on," Dennis told her, "let's go inside."

So they went into the shop and Sonia tried on bracelets and some rings too. Dennis then put his arms around her and told her how he'd love to buy her one, but could not afford it at that time. She simply smiled saying that just that thought was enough for her, and she just wanted him to stay close to her constantly. He then replied to her saying how in his mind he wished he could freeze time, and never let that day come to an end, because he wanted her to stay close to him always. The music playing over the mall speakers at that moment was a beautiful song, **(25) "In Loving You" (Junior English)** the words of which were the perfect sentiment for how they were both feeling. They were really happy to be together again and they knew that nothing would ever come between the love they felt for each other. Sonia asked the shop assistant if it would possible to use their rest room. She was shown the way which was around the corner behind the counter. When she returned, she noticed that Dennis had a big grin on his face, but when she asked him about it, he said it was nothing. It puzzled her for a moment, but then she wondered how the others were getting on in the toy shop, and when they walked in they saw that Patsy had found a nice colourful ball with the words, 'Reggae Boyz' on it. She asked Sonia if she thought her brother would like it.

"Lukie likes anything to do with football," Sonia informed her, "I'm sure he'll love it."

So, Patsy bought the ball, and as they all left the air conditioned mall back into the afternoon heat heading for the car, they heard someone calling out to them from a taxi. They turned to see that it was aunty Ruby, wanting to know what they were all doing in Kingston, after they had only just arrived the day before. Everything was explained to her, after which she invited them all to her house to meet her family and to have something to eat before they returned home. It was an invitation gladly accepted as they were all getting a bit hungry by that time. Ruby was laughing out loud telling them how she had only gone out to pay a bill at her bank, and thought she was seeing things when she saw them all come out of the mall.

The taxi was the same one she had taken to collect them the previous day from the airport; Duggy Fresh seemed to be her personal taxi service. So, Dennis followed him to her home, which was a three bed town house in the Fort Charles area of Stoney Hill. It had a good size front drive, featuring two beautiful dwarf coconut trees and enough space which could hold three cars comfortably. There was a well designed welcoming central veranda with rooms to both sides and, as Duggy Fresh pulled away giving a friendly beep on his horn, Ruby took her guests inside her beautiful home.

Her daughter, Dominique, came downstairs when her mother called her to meet her family from England, and their friends. Then, once they'd all got acquainted, she told the girls about her wedding that was bearing down on her and a problem she was having with her wedding dress. Dennis and Troy were glad when Ruby took them to relax on the back patio and offered them a couple of cool beers, while the girls were deep in wedding talk. The patio overlooked a swimming pool and several fruit trees on a well tended property.

While the brothers enjoyed a quiet moment admiring the garden, inside the house the girls were trying to see if there was anything they could do to assist Dominique with her problem. It turned out that the bridal shop from where she had bought the dress had gone out of business and so there was no way she could get the dress altered. It needed altering because of a little weight she had gained since buying the dress over a year before in the sales. The job could have been done by another bridal shop, but the cost they were asking for was extortionate; and anyway their budget for the wedding was fast running out.

Patsy looked at Sonia and said to Dominique, "Maybe if

you had someone who was a brilliant dress designer and a whizz on a sewing machine, they'd be able to help."

Sonia knew what her cousin was thinking, and right away admitted to Dominique, "I don't know about the brilliant bit, but I am a designer, and using a sewing machine is second nature to me, all thanks to my beloved grandmother who taught me, and I would love to help you."

Dominique was overjoyed when Sonia told her this and, after informing the boys that they would be busy upstairs for while, all three girls set to work on the dress. As neither Dominique or her mother owned a sewing machine, they resorted to asking a neighbour if they could borrow theirs. After that hurdle, it only took Sonia a couple of hours to sort out the alteration and the end result saw Dominique in her wedding dress that fitted just perfectly.

Ruby's husband, Tony, came home in the late afternoon to find a house full of people, and was pleased to meet everyone. Ruby had been the perfect host by firstly, making sandwiches plus bun and cheese for her hungry guests, and then secondly, preparing a family meal. This consisted of brown stew chicken with rice and gungo peas, along with green bananas and yams. All of that would be washed down with a glass of Guinness punch.

During the meal, various subjects were discussed including granny Henni's funeral, Dominique's now fixed wedding dress, and also Dennis' music plans. But when Patsy mentioned her working for the Intercontinental Hotel on Park Lane, Tony was well impressed, because he also worked for the Intercontinental Hotels Group. He was the Operations Manager of the Holiday Inn Sunspree resort in Montego Bay.

"I've been there for three years now," he told her. "It can get quite busy with over 500 suites to cater for, but I enjoy the work."

"You must have an organised crew in the restaurants there I should imagine," Patsy remarked.

"Yes, I've a great team who always goes the extra mile to please our guests," Tony replied, and then he continued, "you know, Patsy, if you ever want to return to Jamaica, I'm sure we could arrange a transfer for you to use your experience at our resort in Mobay anytime you wish."

"Don't tempt me," she smiled. "I may just take you up on that offer some day."

They all had a good laugh about it and then the doorbell rang.

"I think it must be my fiancé," said Dominique. "I'll go see."

She was right. It was her fiancé, Patrick, who had arrived to take her out for the evening to their friend's engagement party.

After introducing him to her new friends and relations, she asked them, "Do you guy's wanna' come to the party? Don't worry about an invite, it's my girl Sharon's engagement and all my friends are her friends too."

Dominique had a style that was infectiously welcoming. Dennis looked worryingly at his watch and said that if they did go, they couldn't stay too long. He reminded them all about his flight the next day, but Sonia gave him a reassuring smile and told him not to worry; she would make sure they left in good time.

They were all excited about going to the party, and Dominique took the girls upstairs to freshen themselves up, while the guys talked with Patrick and Tony in the lounge at the front of the house.

Ruby was in the kitchen tidying up after dinner and loading the dishwasher while listening to the Monday evening news on TVJ from a little portable television she had out there. "Lord have mercy," she thought to herself when she heard the news report about a pig farmer in May Pen refusing to move the animal enclosure from the front of the yard, with its unbearable smells and ensuing complaints from the neighbours. There was a Justice of the Peace trying to encourage him to move the smelly problem to the rear of the yard, but he was having none of it.

"Ah you a go pay the bill fi move it?" was his question to the JP.

"Only in Jamaica!" Ruby said out loud, smiling and shaking her head. "Only in Jamaica!"

She thought about her younger brother, Gordon, who she hoped would be coming over from New York for the wedding. What she had just heard would be a good joke to relate to him when she next called him up. Aside from him, she only had one long lost older sister, named Leonie, whose whereabouts was uncertain ever since running away from the family to get married to someone their parents disapproved of. They had been very outspoken anti-colonialists, and Ruby still remembered the arguments Leonie had with them about her English boyfriend in Kingston. She recalled her sister telling her once, how she wished aunt Miriam, their mother's youngest sister, was their mother; because she would be sure to let her live her life free without any kind of pressure about who she can or can't fall in love with. At the time, Ruby was just a young teenager with no understanding of the power of true love, and their little brother, Gordon, was only eight. He always used to run to Leonie after she'd had an argument with their parents, and was looking sad. Well, wherever she was, Ruby and Gordon always held on to the hope of one day seeing their big sister again.

After a short time, the three girls came down looking real good and the boys were pleased to see their smiling faces. They all waved goodbye to Tony and Ruby as their cars headed away in the direction of Bellamy Heights, a new housing district in New Kingston.

# CHAPTER 10
## ENGAGEMENT PARTY

It was around 7pm when they arrived at Sharon's house, and the party was already rocking with music from a sound system set up in the back garden. The first song they heard playing was a beautiful love song called **(26) "Feel The Feeling" (Bob Andy)**. No one could be seen dancing in the middle of the candle lit garden, but there were a few couples enjoying a slow dance by the garden walls, showing everyone how they felt for each other. Unlike Dominique, Patrick was never one to show his feelings in public or show off about his love for her, but she knew him well enough not to worry about it. His true feelings for her ran deep, just like the song **(27) "Still Waters Run Deep" (The Mighty Diamonds)** which was the next record being played by the DJ.

When Dominique and Sharon saw each other, there first commenced some crazy girly screams, followed by heated, excited hugs. Patrick was well used to this ritual by the girls, and when they'd finished, everyone got introduced. Sharon and her fiancé Paul were very pleased to meet Dominique's family and friends from St Thomas and England. It was the beginning of an unforgettable evening.

The DJ was keeping the party bubbling with some real good Lovers Rock tracks. When he noticed that Dennis Bowen was actually there at the party, he beckoned him over to sing one of his songs. Dennis tried resisting the offer, as he was enjoying dancing with his girl so much, but when Sharon came over and begged him to do one song just for her and Paul's engagement, how could he refuse?

He told Sonia to hold on as he took the microphone and said, "This song is dedicated to Sharon and Paul, Dominique and Patrick, and also to all the other lovers out there tonight, including my brother Troy and Patsy, and especially to my girl Sonia, to whom I do promise to give every beat of my heart... *if she'll have me!!!*"

# ENGAGEMENT PARTY

The song was called **(28) "One In A Million" (Sanchez).**

As Dennis sang the beautiful love song, Sonia could not believe she had just been proposed to, but she already knew the answer would be yes.

"So, Miss wire waist, what's your reply?" asked Dennis, as the song ended.

With the whole crowd waiting with baited breath, she hugged her man, and with tears of joy she whispered, "Yes."

Then Patsy said, "Louder, we couldn't hear you."

"Yes!,Yes!,Yes!," Sonia shouted out for the whole world to hear.

Dennis then reached into his pocket and presented her with a little blue box, similar to one that they had seen earlier that day in the jewellery shop. When she opened up the spring loaded top, there inside was a beautiful gold and diamond engagement ring - the very one she had loved when she had tried it on. She smiled as she remembered his grinning after she had come out from the rest room, and realized what he must have done in those few minutes. The ring fitted perfectly and it truly was a perfect end to one very perfect day.

With all the excitement of the evening, the time had just flown by and it was Troy who had to remind his brother about his flight the following afternoon. Sonia was still beaming with delight as she and Patsy talked about her surprised engagement.

"Come on guys," beckoned Dennis, "We've really got to be going."

It was 11pm by the time they had said their goodbyes to their new friends. They had all exchanged contact details and promised to keep in touch. Dominique said that both she and Patrick would try and make it to the funeral.

"Oh, I do hope you can," Sonia replied, "we'd love to see you guys again before we return to England."

As they drove away, they could still hear the music from the party filling the night air. The song they could hear was **(29) "After Tonight" (Matumbi)** and Sonia thought about the words, agreeing that indeed Dennis was her key to set her free, and after that night everything would be alright.

During the ride home, Troy told Patsy he had enjoyed her company that day, and that he'd be seeing her next at the funeral. She replied saying that she was really looking forward to seeing him there. At around midnight, the girls were dropped off and the boys waved goodbye as they headed home to get some sleep. But there was no sleep on the agenda for Sonia, nor for anyone else in the house, because she woke up the household announcing her engagement to Dennis. Her mother could not believe what she was hearing as the girls related the whole day's exciting events. There were offers of congratulations from everyone, and Patsy's father opened a bottle of champagne to toast the occasion. Aunt Valerie was on top form when it came to informing Sonia on the merits of finding a good man and making sure he knows how to look after a woman. She certainly had not earned the unspoken nickname 'big mouth Valerie' for nothing.

"Why didn't he stop by for a while Sonia?" asked aunt Ethel, as her brother poured out the drinks.

Sonia explained that Dennis couldn't stop as he had to get some rest for the midday flight, but added that they'd be able to catch up with him in the morning, before he goes to the airport. All the noisy commotion woke Lukie, who entered the lounge asking Patsy if she'd remembered his present. She smiled and handed him the football, which he was very pleased to receive.

Everyone was intrigued as they listened to everything that they had manage to pack into that one day, including the wonderful way Dennis had proposed, and also Patsy and Troy's new friendship too.

The next morning, Dennis stopped by to say goodbye to Sonia and the others. Sandra congratulated him and welcomed him into the family.

"Steady on," chuckled Marcus. "They're not married yet!"

"Well, I don't care," came her smiling reply, "I'm welcoming him in anyway."

After a long time saying goodbye to Sonia by the gate, Dennis got into his taxi, which then turned and headed out for the airport. As she watched him disappear from view, Sonia thought about the last thing they had just discussed, which was about meeting up again in London in a week or two after the funeral; and they both could not wait.

# ENGAGEMENT PARTY

Well, the flight to London was on time and Dennis met up with his band mates at Heathrow's arrivals hall on Wednesday morning. He certainly had a lot to tell them on the way to their hotel, and they could not believe that in just three days he had got himself engaged.

"Wow, man!" smiled Norman, "you didn't waste any time did you?"

"When you know you've got the right woman, there's no need to hang around boys," Dennis replied, confidently.

All three friends had a great evening in the hotel bar that night, celebrating Dennis' engagement.

On Friday, the tour kicked off at London's Lyceum Ballroom in Wellington Street, just off the Strand. Dennis and the boys wowed the crowd with hit after hit, so that by the time Bob and his crew came on, everyone was feeling really good. It was a tremendous night, full of good vibes with people dancing in the aisles; how can anyone be seated when such fantastic music was playing?

Bob, having heard about Dennis' engagement, had prepared a surprise for him that night. After he'd gone about half way through his set, he announced that Dennis from 'The Grovans' had recently got engaged to his long-time girlfriend, Sonia, in Jamaica and he wanted to dedicate the next song to both of them. The song was **(30) "Satisfy My Soul" (Bob Marley)**.

Dennis, watching from the side of the stage, was awestruck at the announcement and he gave Bob two thumbs up as he watched them perform the song. The audience were in rapturous applause and Dennis could not wait to tell Sonia all about it.

# CHAPTER 11
## GOODBYE GRANNY

Meanwhile, back in Jamaica on the evening when Dennis was flying over to London, Sandra could see that her daughter was feeling sad about her fiancé leaving. So they both sat down in the lounge and talked about him and her engagement.

"Oh, Sonia, I'm so happy for you." Sandra told her, "It's such a shame your father was not here to see his big girl get engaged."

"I know mum," replied Sonia. "I'm gonna telephone him tonight and tell him all about it."

"He'll be so pleased," her mother added, "and he'll be

the happiest father walking you down the aisle."

They both laughed heartily at the thought, and then Sonia remembered someone else who would have been happy for her too; her granny Henni. Sandra agreed that her mother would have been delighted at the prospect of Sonia getting wed.

"You know, she actually mentioned Dennis by name a few times in her letters to me when you were with her many years ago," Sandra revealed. "Yes, she said he was a lovely boy who was your special friend at school."

"Oh, mum, I know for sure that she really did like Dennis," Sonia replied, crying on her mother's shoulder, "and it's so sad she can't be here."

Aunt Ethel overheard the conversation and exclaimed, "That's why we're going to make sure she has a great send off."

"Yes, that's right!" Sonia agreed, in a more cheerful spirit.

And as Patsy entered the room with her mother, aunt Ethel said to all of them, "Come on girls, we've got lots to organize for the funeral."

Later that same week, Dominique phoned informing Sonia that, although her mum would be coming, unfortunately she and Patrick would be unable to attend the funeral. However, she wished that everything would go well on the day. Sonia had replied, telling her not to worry as she knew they had a lot to do with their wedding coming up and everything. Dominique appreciated her understanding and then had jokingly added that if they didn't have to return to England so soon, they would have been welcomed to gate-crash their wedding. Sonia had just smiled at the thought.

"You guys are having so much fun out here," Dominique had remarked. "Why don't you just come back home and settle down in our island paradise?"

"Dominique!" Sonia shouted, while smiling too. "You make it sound so simple."

"Well, it's just a thought that occurred to me when you got engaged to Dennis," Dominique had replied. "And I'm sure we'd all have a great time out here, but I'll just leave you with that thought. Bye for now and all the best for your big day."

After that phone call, Sonia could not get the idea

out of her head about returning home to Jamaica; the beautiful island paradise that it was. She remembered her granny's wise words to her the day before leaving for England.

"Yes, granny," she thought to herself. "Life is what *you* make it."

She discussed it with Patsy over dinner, and slowly the idea grew and grew until they both were sure that there really was nothing stopping them returning home. After all, Patsy could work for Dominique's father at the resort in Montego Bay, and Sonia could easily start a business in chic fashion if she put her mind to it. And to start off with a place to live, Dennis could give up his apartment and they could stay in granny's house, which was going to be empty once everyone had returned home after the funeral.

When they told the rest of the family about their plans, everyone was pleased for them and wished them both success. The one person who was most pleased to hear it was Dennis. He had phoned the house a few days after arriving in London and couldn't believe his ears when Sonia told him about it. It was the best news he'd heard and told her he couldn't wait to be together as husband and wife. Patsy could not wait to let Troy hear the news, and so she and Sonia took a taxi over to his place one evening to tell him. Jasmine and Derek were pleased to see them and they all had a lovely time. Troy told Patsy that it was a brilliant decision, one he'd make sure she would never regret. The two of them were as happy as two people falling in love could ever be.

By the following week, the funeral arrangements were all in order. There was to be refreshments available afterwards at the house for all the guests, which Patsy was in charge of. She had both vegetable, and cow foot soup for starters, followed by the main meal consisting of rice and peas, which would be served with a choice of curried goat or brown stew chicken. In addition to all that would be fried fish, ackee and salt-fish, salad, coleslaw and festivals.

On the day of the funeral, everyone got ready for the 11am service that would be followed by the burial in a family plot, at the Red Hills cemetery in Morant Bay. When grandpa Rensford had passed away, a double plot made sense, as granny Henni had made it known that she wanted to be buried with him when her time came, and they were told that available burial spaces at that cemetery were running low.

Aunty Ruby was there, decked out in her best black dress, and wide netted hat. Sandra and her two sisters were weeping as the coffin was lowered down by the cemetery workers, painfully reminding them of their father's funeral which they had also attended back in 1971. Sonia, Patsy, and Hazel could not hold back the tears either as the Minister read Psalm 23 from his Bible. Marcus and George, together with Derek and Troy, as well as some of the other men in attendance, took turns with shovelling the piled up red soil into the deep pit until there was a raised mound. At this point the women took over, decorating it with flowers and fancy borders. Jasmine and her mother, Grace, helped, along with Ena too, and when they had all finished, it looked really beautiful, with lots of photos being taken of it.

Slowly, everyone made their way from there to granny's house for the prepared refreshments. There were people in every corner of the house and all over the yard too.

By then, Lukie was feeling hot and hungry, and exclaimed, "Aunt Patsy, when is the food going to be ready?"

Sandra, looking slightly embarrassed, told him, "Not

long Lukie, and anyway it's not like you didn't have any breakfast this morning."

Patsy smiled at Lukie and whispered quietly to him, "Never mind Lukie, I'll make sure you are first in the queue."

There was a little laughter following Lukie's outburst, and then all attention turned to Troy, who as the DJ for the occasion, had just put on the first record which was **(31) "Tune In" (Gregory Isaacs).** Sonia had given him a list of songs granny Henni would have liked and that was one love song that she remembered her granny singing along to. Troy continued playing similar light background reggae music as the food was served, and later he and Patsy had enjoyed getting to know each other even better in the relaxed atmosphere. Dennis' grandmother, Grace, was talking to Sonia about him and Troy, and some of the tricky things they used to get up to when they were kids staying with her in Portland. She also mentioned an occasion when she first met granny Henni who had come to Port Antonio to buy supplies in the wholesalers for her business. The two boys had nearly knocked her off her feet with their chasing around, and Grace had ordered them to apologize; which they did sheepishly. Sonia enjoyed hearing the tales, and also thanked her for wishing them a happy marriage.

Well, the funeral for granny Henni was a success and everyone remarked how well it had all been organized; not to mention the food which was top notch. She had been a well loved member of the community and this had been reflected in the number of people who came to show such a dear lady their last respects.

A few days later, Valerie and Ethel were the first to leave and return to their families in the United States. In New York, Bert would be welcoming home Valerie; and in Miami, Carlton was waiting patiently on Ethel's return. Before leaving, the two aunts had wished their nieces all the best for their future plans and hoped to see them all again soon.

# CHAPTER 12
## RETURNING RESIDENTS

Before going back to the UK after the funeral, Sonia and Patsy had a few days to start organising their plans for returning home to JA. Patsy telephoned Dominique's dad to take him up on his offer of a job in his hotel. He told her that it was no problem; as soon as she was ready there would be a job waiting for her there. She was really happy to hear him confirm his promise that way.

When Dominique heard about their returning back to Jamaica plans, she was ecstatic and told Sonia she would try to find a position for her in one of her friends fashion outlets in Kingston if she got stuck for work.

Sonia didn't know what to say at such a kind offer, "Thanks Dominique, you are a true friend"

Two days before he returned to Canada with Ena, Marcus accompanied the girls and his brother to an appointment with the Ministry of Foreign Affairs in Kingston. They wanted to find out if there was any important information that returning residents to Jamaica needed to know.

The meeting was very informative and they were told that under the laws of Jamaica, they could be considered to be a Returning Resident, and thereby be eligible to concessions relating to personal and household effects, as long as they met three main criteria. Firstly, they had to be a Jamaican national who had reached the age of eighteen years of age. Secondly, they must have been resident overseas for not less than three consecutive years. And thirdly, they must be returning to Jamaica in order to reside permanently.

As both Sonia and her cousin satisfied all those conditions, the officer told them he wished them all the best with their plans and that they could call his office anytime if they needed help with anything else.

So everything was set in motion for the day to come when they would be returning home and nothing was going to stop them. First though, they had to get back to London, so everyone got packed and ready for their flight home.

At the airport, Troy and Patsy were saying long goodbyes, but they knew it would not be too long before they would be together again. Suddenly, Troy overcome with emotion, took her to a private corner near the entrance to the airport. Patsy was in a daze and wondered what was going on.

Troy then got down on one knee and said, "Patsy, I want you to know how much I care for you and how I hate to see you leave like this. I really love you girl, and Patsy, will...will you marry me?"

Patsy was taken aback by Troy's proposal and didn't know how to respond. Sure she was attracted to him from the moment they'd met, but marriage, it seemed to be going a bit too fast. Her response to him was in the words of a song that really summed up what she was thinking. The song was **(32) "Keep It Like It Is" (Louisa Mark).** She really needed some time to consider if she was to accept his offer. So she told him it might be better if they just kept things as they were for the time being. Troy accepted her honesty, and told her she could take as long as she wanted to make a decision about marriage. They walked back slowly and rejoined the others. When Sonia and everyone else asked them where they'd been, Patsy smiled and told them not to worry, they were just saying goodbye. She then looked at Sonia and whispered that she would tell her what had really happened later during the flight. Hazel and Sandra took a knowing look at each other, certain that there was more to it than simply saying goodbye. But they were sure that before they reached London they would know anyway; these girls could never keep anything quiet.

It was another extremely hot and sunny afternoon in Kingston as the Air Jamaica jet taxied down the runway. The illuminated signs overhead read, 'FASTEN SEAT BELTS,' after which the cabin crew had gone through the usual safety routine and were now seated, ready for take off.

Troy watched as the plane's engines started to roar, taking it from standstill to over 200 miles per hour. Within no time they were on their way to London.

No sooner had they been airborne, when Patsy told them all about her declining of Troy's proposal. Her mother told her that she thought it was the right decision and that she'd have plenty of time to really get to know Troy when she returned home to JA. Sonia was happy for her because at last there was someone who really cared for her, unlike the others in her past. Patsy knew she was right but could not help wondering if she had indeed made the right decision.

Lukie was holding onto his mother's hand and asking if they really had to go back so soon; he had really enjoyed it in Jamaica.

Patsy was thinking about Troy, and Sonia's mind was on Dennis. Two cousins had fallen for two brothers and everything in their futures looked bright. After all, they were all going to be living in Jamaica; what better place could there be than a paradise island with love as the key to set you free.

# CHAPTER 13
## TWO WILL ALWAYS BE ONE

To complete their UK tour, Bob Marley performed two final nights at London's Lyceum Ballroom, the same venue where it had all started from. The four week tour which ended mid February had been a triumph, and 'The Grovans' were a critically acclaimed supporting act.

Dennis had organized free tickets for Sonia, Patsy, and their family, plus a backstage pass for one. He was pleased to show off his girl to the other guys, Bob and the Wailers, and the I-Three's too.

"So, when are you two getting hitched?" Bob asked straight out.

"Soon, man," Dennis replied, smiling, "we're getting married in Jam-down."

Bob wished them success in their marriage and then he thanked everyone for a great tour. He told them all that they were just the best.

After all that backstage well wishing, Dennis told the guys he'd meet them back at the hotel later, as he was taking Sonia for a late night stroll along the Strand. Patsy and the other members of the family had already gone home after the show, when Dennis had taken Sonia backstage with him.

Dennis asked her if she would like something to eat, to which she replied that she would love a Big Mac. He fancied one himself, so they ventured out into the cold night, and after walking down past a few shops, they saw a McDonald's restaurant by Charing Cross station. That particular branch was usually frequented by people waiting for their train, but as it was around 11pm there weren't that many customers. Once inside, they ordered two Big Macs with fries and strawberry shakes, then sat down by the window observing the London night life outside as they relaxed in each others company. They had to make the most of the next few days because Dennis was going to be returning to Jamaica with the band to record their new single; the half written song he had collected from his apartment and managed to complete on the tour. It was all about a guy knowing that a girl fancies him, even though she's trying to hide it. Its title is **(33) "I Know The Score" (Frankie Paul).** Dennis sang the song quietly to her, and then she smiled, telling him she thought it sounded like it would be another hit for them.

They left the restaurant and walked on for a while, huddled close and holding hands, looking at shops and old buildings steeped in history. Sonia noticed an antique shop across the road with African artefacts on display in the window. It seemed interesting and so they crossed the road for a closer look. The items were much clearer now and they had a good look for a while. There were some spears and masks, also beaded necklaces and chains. It was all quite colourful and beautiful to look at, and after a few minutes they turned to leave. However, just as they were about to go, Sonia noticed a piece of silver jewellery. It was very similar to the silver bangle given to her by her granny, and which she still was wearing; in fact to Sonia it seemed identical. She told Dennis that she would love to buy it as a present for him, but as the shop was closed she would have to return in the morning to buy it. For a moment she wondered if it could in any way be linked to the story of the African bangle in her family's history, but dismissed it straight away as nonsense.

"What were you thinking about just then?" asked Dennis with a puzzled smile.

"Oh, just something I remembered my granny told me about my bangle," Sonia replied, at which she proceeded to tell him the handed down story surrounding her bangle.

He was fascinated to hear it, and was deep in thought as they walked away. There was a cab approaching, which stopped after being hailed by Dennis. First he dropped her off home, then onwards to his hotel.

It had been so nice being with her fiancé again, and Sonia had told him how her father was looking forward to meeting him, now the tour had ended. They were both going up to Bristol the following Tuesday, and after that she knew it would be goodbye again until their wedding in September.

The next morning, following their late night stroll,

Sonia returned to the antique shop. On entering the premises, the owner, a well dressed elderly man in his sixties, welcomed her in. She asked to see the bangle in the window and, after he brought it to her, he noticed the one she had on was very similar and asked where she got hers from. Sonia told him that it was a present from her grandmother in Jamaica. As he handed her the requested item, she scrutinized the markings on it, which were also the same inscription as on hers and wondered what the chances would be of her finding the actual second bangle as told by her family's old stories. Sonia was getting very excited at what she thought she may have discovered and asked him how it came to be in his possession.

The man then said it was all very intriguing, and proceeded to tell her why. Apparently, his African artefacts business offered pawn brokering services too, and an old West Indian woman had pawned her bangle to him. However, she had never returned to claim it within the six months redemption period, nor during the three months of grace following that. He had really felt sure she would be coming back for it, but reluctantly decided to put it out on display; which was the same day that Sonia had seen it.

When Sonia had asked why he felt so sure she would be coming back to claim it, he had then proceeded to tell her what the woman had told him about the history of the bangle: During a short time in Africa, she had unwittingly discovered the story of the original owner who was a princess from a West African tribe called Mantogo. She had been promised in marriage to the son of a tribal lord from another village, and as part of her dowry, a unique set of two bangles were commissioned and given to her to wear. Translated, the markings on the outside reads, 'Two Will Always Be One.' It was a metaphor for the young princess, meaning that she and her husband would stay married forever and the two bangles would also reflect that by always being together on her wrist. Sadly, shortly before the wedding, the young bride to be was kidnapped and sold into slavery!

Unknown to anyone was the fact that the bangles were separated when the slave ship captain forcefully took one off her, while allowing her to keep the other. However, he later forfeited it in India during a late night gambling session. Then throughout the following two centuries, it continued being owned by various people; from the subcontinent all the way to Liverpool. And it was there in 1925, that its latest owner, a railway engineer, went on to present it as a third year anniversary gift to his young wife.

Continuing the old woman's tale, the pawnbroker said she'd stated how she had been a former coffee waitress at the Kingston railway terminus, in Jamaica, which was where she first met her husband, an engineer from England. She had also divulge that they had been forced to run away from her village to get married, due to her parent's anti-colonialist stance. The pawnbroker smiled as he told Sonia that it was clear to him that she did not regret her actions, as it seemed to have been done all in the name of love. He then added that the woman had no idea as to the whereabouts of the other bangle.

The slave princess had obviously treasured her one remaining bangle as the only connection to her past life which had been so brutally ripped from her. Later on, as she had struggled with life on the plantation, she would pass on that bangle and its history to her family, as they subsequently did onto theirs.

Thus the two bangles had lost their connection. But now, incredibly, they had found themselves again!

To hear that story, and to think of the history

behind the two bangles, left Sonia amazed and speechless. It all tied up with the stories handed down by her own family. She told the pawnbroker that she could now understand why he was so sure the old woman would have returned to redeem it. Who could she be?... and where was she now?... Sonia asked for her address, but due to data protection laws, he was unable to comply with her wishes. She did, however, leave him her first name and her family's Bristol address, in case the woman ever returned and wanted to get in touch.

Well, at least she could buy the bangle for Dennis, which was her main task for that morning. The price tag was £85, which she gladly paid, and then left the shop after bidding the kind man farewell. On the way home she kept thinking about it, and just couldn't wait to tell her family all that she'd been told, as she was sure they'd be amazed as she was; and that certainly was the case. On hearing the tale, Patsy's father then said something vague about it sounding like the 'runaway and her railway man,' which had reference to more old family stories he remembered being told as a boy. He couldn't recall the story very well, though, so everyone imagined that he was mixing up some old film he might have seen long ago, and they laughed it off as typical of his humorous nature. But whoever she was, they agreed that she had enabled their family's story to be known more clearly.

On their coach journey to Bristol, a few days later, Dennis was looking forward to meeting his future father in law for the first time. Half way there, Sonia related to Dennis all about Leon, just so everything was clear and in the open. He reassured her, telling her that she was entitled to have anyone who she wanted as her friend and she shouldn't feel bad. She was really pleased that he took it that way.

After that, she presented Dennis with the bangle, together with the full story of her visit to the antique shop. Dennis really loved it and he wasted no time in putting it on, telling her how to him it would be a pre-wedding symbol of their love. He meant that especially for the fact that they'd discovered it together when they were not looking for it, yet there it was staring at them in the window. It was just the same as the love they had for each other; they were not looking for it, so many years ago, but there it was staring at them.

Things had turned out just the way granny Henni had said when telling Dennis that she believed the two of them were made for each other. Yes, everything had come full circle; first, granny Henni had given Sonia the silver bangle, and now Sonia had given Dennis it's unique partner; it was simply perfect.

# CHAPTER 14
## DANCE CRUEL

When they arrived at the Bristol Coach Station, Garbert was there to collect them. Sonia introduced him to Dennis and they hit it off straight away as they drove home. Garbert told him he liked his band's music and that one day he'd love to see them playing live. As they parked up outside the house, which was a double bay fronted 1930's built property, Dennis asked him about his work, and Garbert explained how he had been made redundant at the flour mills where he'd worked since coming to this country. But he was not upset about it because the package he received meant he had fulfilled his main wish in life, which was never to be a poor man again. When he said that, he gave a hearty laugh, to which the others could not help but join in with. Sandra came out to the car, wondering what all the joviality was about.

When Garbert told her, she just smiled saying, "I should have guessed; you know Sonia, he's been saying that everyday since he received his redundancy payout."

"Then what do you want me to do?" Garbert retorted, with a glint in his eye, "keep quiet, like mi lose mi tongue?"

It was clear that he was not going to keep his new upgraded financial status to himself, so it would be no point in Sandra even trying. Dennis found it all quite amusing and took warmly to his future father in law.

Inside their home, Sandra told Dennis he'd be sharing Lukie's bedroom, and asked the youngster to showed him the way. Dennis put down his luggage and noticed that a camp bed, which looked very comfortable, had been neatly made up for him by the window. Sonia would be staying in her old bedroom, reminding her of the first years when she arrived in England.

Sandra and Lukie were both happy to meet Dennis

again, since they were all together in Jamaica back in January. Lukie asked him how long he was going to stay.

"Well, Lukie, I'm here for two days," Dennis replied, "so would you like me and your big sis to take you to the park across the road right now?"

"Yes, please," Lukie exclaimed, with boyish excitement, "I'll get my ball that aunty Patsy gave me."

While he was getting it, his mother told them not to stay too long as dinner was nearly ready.

"Ok mum," Sonia replied. "We'll be back soon."

When Lukie came out with his ball, he took hold of his sister's hand to cross the main road over to Eastville Park. Dennis thought how very fortunate they were to have such a clean and well kept park so close to their home.

At the park, Sonia wanted to show Dennis the lake, which was really a beautiful sight, with swans and ducks all around near a large island in the middle. Lukie actually got too close to the edge when he ran over to some little ducklings that had come near to them. Dennis was quick to grab him though, before anything disastrous happened. Following that close incident, Sonia suggested they go up to the swings where Lukie would be safer, and he could play with his ball, which was what they originally planned to do anyway. This they did and had a good time playing headers.

When they got back, it was around 5pm, and time for dinner. Sandra had prepared stew peas made with pigs tails, served with rice. It was one of her husband's favourite meals. He always commended her, saying it was just like his mama used to make.

During the meal, their conversations drifted from wedding plans, where they would live, Sonia's work outlook, and Patsy and Troy's future plans too. Garbert had made it clear that if they ever needed anything financially, he'd be there for them and they told him that they really appreciated his offer.

Sonia had also mentioned about the story of their bangles, and about her uncle George's strange remarks. She asked her mum if she knew what her brother may have had in mind. Then, after thinking about it for a while, Sandra recalled the family story she'd also heard as a little girl, just like her brother. It was about one of her mum's nieces who had ran away to get married with an English railwayman, way way back; and from that day nothing was heard of her again. This made Sonia take a deep breath, thinking that maybe, just maybe the old woman was related to them. Whether or not that was true, Sonia said it was the nearest answer they had to solving the riddle, and maybe one day they would know for sure.

They had also talked about going out to the pub for the evening if Sandra could get a babysitter for Lukie. That wouldn't be a problem; there was a sixteen old girl called Tracey who usually helped out. She was the daughter of a neighbour of theirs, living two doors down from them, who had always loved playing with Lukie from when he was born. Sonia remembered Tracey as a freckle faced, ginger haired twelve year old, when she first arrived in England, always coming round and asking to hold the baby. Well, Tracey remained a good friend to Lukie, and Sandra trusted her to be a good babysitter whenever she needed one.

At nine o'clock, Tracey arrived when everyone was just about set to go out. Sandra told her they would be back before midnight and to help herself to crisps and juice in the fridge.

The pub, called 'The Four Blackbirds,' was just around the corner, so they did not need to drive. As they approached the door, they could hear loud reggae music emanating from within. Once inside, they passed a group of men playing dominoes with such force, it was a wonder the pieces did not shatter. Just then, some of Garbert's friends called over to him and he went over and introduced them to his family.

While this was going on, Dennis noticed that most of the people in the crowded pub were focussing their attention on an elderly man, who was dancing with a much younger woman, near the sound system in the corner. They were dancing to a song called **(34) "To Love Someone" (Paul Dawkins)**.

One or two other couples were dancing too, but if it was a dance-off there was no doubt who the winners were. All eyes were fixed on them; the man in his seventies doing some real cool moves with the woman who looked to be in her fifties, wearing a light blue chiffon evening dress, with shiny patent black stilettos. He was wearing a cream coloured suit, blue shirt with a red tie, and a brown trilby sporting a single white feather.

Garbert took his family to an unoccupied round

table with four chairs and obtained their orders. When he returned with the drinks, Dennis asked him who the old guy doing the cool dancing was.

"That's my old friend Jordan Pynes, also known as 'Dance Cruel,'" he told him. "The 'cruellest' dancer in Bristol."

"Well," Dennis started, with a joking smile, "his name certainly fits his game."

All, except Sandra, smiled as they sipped their drinks. She looked askance, kissing her teeth, saying, "I wonder what his wife, Velma, would say if she saw him dancing like that with that woman?"

To change the subject, Sonia interjected, "Well, that's 'Dance Cruel' and his wife's problem. Tell me mum, whatever happened to Queenie and Leon? I remember you saying, didn't you, that they had emigrated to Canada?"

Then Dennis, having been informed earlier on all about Queenie and Leon, made a joke saying, "Oh, Leon, that was your old flame, right?"

"No, he wasn't, Dennis," Sonia protested, poking him in his side. "He was a friend; that was all, and I told you."

"I know, I know," Dennis responded, softly. "Just kidding."

Sandra answered Sonia, saying, "Queenie is doing fine in Toronto, the last time she wrote. Her husband's brother had sponsored his immigration application and he was granted a permanent residency card a while back. She is really happy to be back with him now, after Leon finally completed his college courses last year."

"Canada," Garbert lit up. "Now that's a place I'd like to visit. Maybe we could take a trip after the wedding and look for them, Sandra, what do you reckon?"

"Yes, I would love to see them again," Sandra agreed, "it would be nice to find out what Canada is really like, and we could stay with my brother, Marcus and his family, who lives near Toronto."

"From what I've heard, it's a great country," expressed Dennis. "I'm sure you'd all love it there."

They continued drinking and talking until about 11pm, when 'Dance Cruel' left the dancing and came over to their table. He shook hands with Garbert who pulled him up a chair and offered him a drink; Bells

Whisky was always his favourite tipple. He seemed pleased to meet Garbert's family, and the two old friends related how they had first met each other at the flour mills when Jordan arrived for his first day there, and Garbert was the one who had to show him the ropes. Jordan had previously worked on the railways, then later after leaving the flour mills he worked as a porter in the Bristol Royal Infirmary, where he stayed until he retired.

Dennis asked Jordan where he had learned to dance so good, and he was told that it all began in Jamaica as a young man, and his moves never left him.

After engaging in conversation with the family for about fifteen minutes, Jordan felt the call of the dance floor when the DJ laid down one of his favourite songs. It was called **(35) "Love Is What You Make It Girl" (Investigators)**. And so, after saying goodbye to Garbert and the others, he returned to the floor as 'Dance Cruel.' Although he now had a different dance partner with him, he had the same unmistakable signature moves that no words could possibly describe. That kind of showmanship just has to be seen to be believed.

Sandra was shaking her head disapprovingly, then

glancing at her watch she told her husband it was about time they should be leaving.

They got back home at 11.45pm, and Sandra asked Tracey how Lukie had been. She was pleased to know that as usual he had been no problem and was tucked up in bed, fast asleep. So Tracey, after saying goodbye to everyone, gave Sandra a hug at the front door before walking the few doors down to her house. Sandra stood watching her by the gate, to make sure she got home safely.

It was the end of a super evening out and before retiring, Sandra asked if anyone wanted a cup of hot chocolate. They all said they would, so the men sat in the lounge watching the telly, while the women made the drinks.

Out in the kitchen, Sonia brought up the subject of 'Dance Cruel' to her mother, "You're not too keen on him, are you mum?"

"Don't bother getting me started on that man, Sonia," she replied, shaking her head. "I work with his wife, Velma, cleaning down at the health centre and she's always complaining to me about him and his antics. She's good to put up with him, I know for sure I wouldn't."

"Oh well, my fault for bringing it up again, but like I said before," Sonia replied. "That problem's for her and him to deal with I guess; come on, let's take in these drinks."

Well, a great time certainly was had in Bristol; the two days flew by, and Dennis had really enjoyed meeting and getting acquainted with his future father in law. He knew he would never forget some of the things he had said, and as they rode on the coach back to London, Sonia and Dennis also knew they would never forget meeting the cool dancer, Jordan Pynes a.k.a 'Dance Cruel.'

It was all too soon before Dennis and his band mates had checked out of their hotel and getting into a taxi bound for the airport. Sonia and Patsy had taken the underground to Heathrow Central station and met them all at the check-in area.

Sonia was really happy to see Dennis again and soon they were kissing goodbye once more. "We must stop saying goodbye like this," Sonia smiled, as she looked deep into his eyes.

"Just hang on in there," was his warm reply. "It'll all

be fine when we are together for good in Jamaica."

Patsy wished Dennis and the other guys a safe flight and remarked how she could not wait to be joining them all soon in sunny JA.

Watching the information screens was Norman, who informed everyone that it was time to go. So, leaving Sonia and her cousin behind, they picked up their hand luggage and headed for the departure lounge. Just before turning the corner out of view, Dennis glanced around him for a final look at his bride to be, blowing her a kiss, which she returned straight away. Then in a moment, they had disappeared from sight!

"Come on, girl," Patsy said, cheerfully. "We've got loads to do, and we've only got seven months to do it in!"

"Yes, I know," agreed Sonia. "I can't wait till it's all over and I'm Mrs Bowen."

"That's got a nice ring to it," laughed Patsy. "Mrs Sonia Bowen."

"And if you marry Troy, you'll be Mrs Bowen too," Sonia reminded her cousin.

"Oh, yes. I hadn't thought of that, Sonia," Patsy replied smiling. "We'll have to watch this space, won't we."

They had a good laugh about it all and then went back to the city by way of the Heathrow Central train station.

## CHAPTER 15
### DOUBLE TROUBLE

Now, as regards their returning to Jamaica plans, the girls had many things arranged within a short time. Sonia had given up her flat, after which she had moved back in with Patsy for the interim. Both of them had handed in notices to their respective employers and were just waiting eagerly for the day to come when they would say goodbye to the UK and hello JA.

The wedding was being organized in Jamaica by Dominique, who had been married for just over three months herself. It was going to be held at her dad's hotel; the Holiday Inn Sunspree resort in Mobay. Both Sonia's and Patsy's families were all coming out for it. All the plans pointed to it being a fantastic wedding on the beach front. Sonia designed her own wedding dress; her sewing skills knew no bounds. Patsy was of course to be her maid of honour, who was so looking forward to the happy occasion of seeing her cousin get married to the man of her dreams. Lukie was excitedly getting prepared for his role as page boy, and Troy as you can guess was to be the best man.

After cutting their new single, Dennis was busy in Jamaica preparing things too, like giving up his Kingston apartment, and getting granny Henni's house freshly decorated by Troy and some other builders. Although it was granny's house, they were going to make it their home. The other family members who the house belonged to did not mind the two of them living in the house as they were family too, and because it was better occupied than left empty. Anyway, all family were free to come and stay for holidays just the same as they had always done when granny was alive.

Earlier, Troy had related to Dennis about his proposal to Patsy, and the advice given was for him not to rush it because good things really do come to those who wait, which was something he could personally testify to. Troy had agreed that he would wait until whenever Patsy was ready.

At last, everything in England had been done and the girls final weeks were bearing down on them. During August, they either took the tube several times to go shopping down central London, or found themselves wandering through Petticoat Lane Market, where they were sure to find cut price fashion clothing and leather accessories. They certainly knew where to find the best bargains to pack for JA.

A farewell party was arranged at Patsy's house in London, and Sonia's family were coming down from Bristol for the special night. It was a typical West Indian house party; lots of food, beer, rum, and loud music. The girls felt really special. They were all having a great time and in the back room a red light bulb had been changed from the normal one, to set the mood for dancing. One record that the girls requested the DJ to play more than once was **(36) "In Love" (Arema)**. "More cut Mr DJ," they'd shout out to him. And like any good DJ 'worth his salt,' he willingly obliged.

At around eleven o'clock the house phone rang. Patsy's dad answered it and recognized that it was

Troy calling long distance. They exchanged greetings, which was difficult with the music so loud in the background, and then Troy asked to speak to Patsy. George told his daughter that Troy was on the phone and that she should take the call upstairs in her mum's bedroom, as that was the quietest place in the house. He had just called to say hello and to let her know how he was missing her. She told him how much she was missing him too and also how good it was to hear his voice, imagining his handsome face with his neatly trimmed goatee. Just by coincidence, the DJ downstairs put on the ideal record for that moment which a song called **(37) "Baby I've Been Missing You" (Bunny Maloney).**

They continued talking for about fifteen minutes and both could not wait to see one another again very soon when she and Sonia returned home to Jamaica. Patsy was sure that if he had proposed to her again that night, she would have said yes in a flash. When she returned to the party, she had a certain glow radiating from her smile that could not hide how she was feeling about her man. For the rest of the evening all she could think of was Troy and being with him again. After the party had finished, she spoke to Sonia and her mum about how she was feeling and how she realized that she had made the wrong decision in not accepting Troy's proposal of marriage. She just wanted to be with him forever. Her mother advised her to follow her heart if that was how she really felt, and Sonia went one step further and told her not to waste time, but to call him back that very night and tell him exactly what she had just told them.

"Remember what granny always told us Patsy," Sonia reminded her. "The only person stopping you from achieving the best in life is *you*."

Patsy agreed with them both and called Troy back to let him know her true feelings. Troy was surprised to get a call from her so soon after they had just spoken a few hours before. However, at the end of the call, everyone was told that she had just accepted Troy's second proposal and a double wedding would need to be organized. The house erupted in excitement and joy.

"Congratulations, cuz," said Sonia, hugging her close. "You two are gonna be so happy, I just know it."

Before they left to go home to Bristol, Sandra and her husband wished Patsy all the very best for her marriage. Lukie asked if he would be her page boy too.

Patsy told him yes, and that he would be the best page boy she could think of. Sonia kissed her parents and little brother goodbye and, after waiving them off, went back inside the house where her aunt was talking.

"But you haven't much time to organize a dress, Patsy," her mother worried, "just two weeks before you leave!"

"Don't worry, mum," was her confident reply, "we'll sort something out, won't we Sonia?"

"Yes, we will," replied Sonia, "everything will be fine, aunty."

Hazel knew they were right, after all from what she'd seen of them organizing their return to Jamaica, her daughter and niece were excellent at getting things done. So she told the girls to go to bed for some well earned rest, and in the morning they could start sorting out these extra new plans.

When they had gone up to bed, Hazel looked at her husband whom she knew was thinking the same things she was. Their only child was not only leaving them soon, but also would be getting married and they would not be there with her after it was all over and they had returned back to England. They talked it over and came to the conclusion that maybe it was time for them to consider returning home themselves, but perhaps they would wait a while to see how Patsy and Troy got on first before deciding.

# CHAPTER 16
## THIS IS LOVERS ROCK

Time was certainly not waiting for anyone, but amazingly the girls had organized everything, including a wedding dress for Patsy.

On their final weekend, they both felt an urge to attend the Notting Hill carnival for the last time. They were looking forward to seeing some of the UK's best Lovers Rock artists, who would be performing live on the Monday night. It was being billed as an unmissable night to remember entitled, 'This Is Lovers Rock.'

The Notting Hill carnival was an event many in the capital's multicultural community looked forward to each year, ever since it got started in 1964, and Sonia and her cousin were no exception. It was the August bank holiday of 1980, and that Monday would be the last day of the weekend spectacular. Along with everyone else, the girls were dressed in their most flamboyant outfits to add to the atmosphere of carnival. They got there early and as they sauntered up and down the crowded streets, full of vendors selling all kinds of food and drinks, they enjoyed the music that filled the air from sound systems which seemed to be pitched on every corner. A procession that included a traditional steel band playing soca music, followed closely by a fantastic display of feather-winged dancers, had been a sight to behold. The crowd of around 200,000 people enjoyed watching the parade as it made its way along Ladbroke Grove, culminating at Great Western Road.

In the late evening, Patsy and Sonia, along with many others, were making their way to the main stage, situated on Westbourne Grove, where the night's special performance had been planned. It had been extensively advertised on colourful flyers pasted all over the place. With the likes of Sandra Cross, Kofi, Louisa Mark, Janet Kay, Carroll Thompson, Matumbi, Junior English, T. T Ross, One Blood, Tradition, Frankie Paul, Wendy Walker, Sugar Minott, and others; it was truly a show not to be missed.

When they got near to the enormous rainbow coloured main stage, they saw Louisa Mark on the platform about to open the show. After performing three of her massive hits, the crowded throng were besides themselves and shouting for more when she left the stage. They certainly weren't disappointed when she returned to give them one more of her top selling songs and this really set the pace for the evening's entertainment that followed.

The artist next on was Jack Wilson, with a wonderful version of one of Louisa Mark's signature tunes. It was **(38) "6 Sixth Street" (Jack Wilson)**. The streets of Notting Hill were rocking to the cool vibes of the fantastic showcase, full of Lovers Rock entertainment.

Each artist in turn kept the crowd dancing with the beautiful music that lovers rock truly is, and to great applause Janet Kay was welcomed onto the stage. She was looking superb in a sporty pair of black leather trousers, and a dazzling white sequinned top. Just at that moment Patsy thought that she recognised a face in the crowd, a face she had not seen for quite some time. Could it be him she thought to herself, the person she'd all but forgotten about?

"Who are you staring at Patsy?" asked Sonia.

"Oh, nothing. I thought I saw Delroy over there just now," came her reply, "but I must have been mistaken."

Patsy was recalling the years that she had wasted with him, and some of the bad ways that he had treated her. She still remembered how he had ignored her on the bus stop with his mum one time, and other occasions when he was just playing with her feelings.

"Anyway," she thought to herself. "He's no match to my Troy, so he'd better not even try."

She had not been mistaken at all because Delroy actually was there with some friends, and after noticing her he was trying to creep up from behind to give her a surprise.

However, as both girls saw him coming up, his surprise was quashed. Sonia looked at Patsy, who just rolled her eyes and shook her head, at the same moment as the song **(39) "Silly Games" (Janet Kay)** started. The words in that song really summed up her feelings at that time towards Delroy. Although she had at one time thought she wanted him, she knew now that he was just a kid who liked playing silly games.

Patsy was quite civil with him though, as she informed him of her plans for a new life in Jamaica, and a husband too. Although he was very surprised to hear all of that, he genuinely wished her all the best for the future, and then he wandered back over to his friends who were beckoning his return.

The girls laughed about the situation and wondered what their life would have been if they had fallen for Delroy and Leon. Sonia said she knew they had both chosen well, and Patsy agreed overwhelmingly.

At around 2am the spotlights shone on Sugar Minott, who was the final artist to perform that night. Everyone saw a smartly dressed man in a white suit preparing to say something. As he stood on the brightly lit platform smiling, he spoke into the microphone in a real silky voice saying, "Ok everyone, this is the final Lovers Rock song tonight." With that, he started singing his most popular track called **(40) "Lovers Rock" (Sugar Minott)**.

Sonia and Patsy had really enjoyed the day and the incredible line-up in the Lovers Rock evening showcase. The last song had really been the perfect one to end the show with.

*  *  *

And so the two lovestruck cousins left the excitement of the carnival streets disappearing behind them as they walked down the steps of the Notting Hill Gate tube station, and onward into their bright futures, with the sound of Lovers Rock still ringing in their ears.

# THE END

# *EPILOGUE*

### *THE WEDDING*

Somewhere on a north coast beach setting in Jamaica, two happy couples repeated their vows in front of family and friends, gathered together on a perfect September afternoon. It had taken a lot of planning and organising to reach that point, but it was all worth it. The two beautiful brides, Sonia and Patsy, looked proud standing beside their two handsomely groomed husbands, Dennis and Troy, as the excited crowd took no ends of photos at the close of the ceremony. Later, during the evening party held in the hotel ballroom, 'The Grovans,' with Dennis included , performed two great songs that everyone enjoyed dancing to, the first of which was **(41) "Rock Away" (Beres Hammond).**

## PATSY AND TROY

Patsy was enjoying her job at the Sunspree resort, and Troy was busy building their house on a plot of land he bought in the Westgate Hills area of Montego Bay. They planned to start a family after around five years.

## SONIA AND DENNIS

Sonia started her own fashion outlet in Morant Bay, utilising her skills acquired from both her granny and her experience from working in England. Her father, Garbert, assisted her financially to start the business, for which she was extremely grateful. Dennis and his band were continuing to be as popular as ever with hit after hit. Both Sonia and Dennis were enjoying life as husband and wife in granny Henni's house.

## HAZEL AND GEORGE

Now as for Hazel and George, they remained in London for five more years before deciding to return home to Jamaica. Patsy and Troy were soon to be having their first child, and they wanted to be be near, as doting grandparents.

# EPILOGUE

## SANDRA AND GARBERT & LUKIE

After the wedding in Jamaica, they went on holiday the following year to visit Sandra's brother, Marcus, and his family in Canada. While there, they also looked for Queenie, her husband, and Leon. As he had stated, Garbert was never a poor man again, and this enabled them to take trips to the United States to visit Sandra's sisters, Ethel and Valerie, and their families. Everyone, including Lukie, enjoyed themselves immensely.

## SHARNETT

Following successful treatment at the Bellevue Hospital, in Kingston, Sharnett was able to cope with her anxieties by maintaining the daily medication prescribed by the doctors. She was back living with her mother in Spanish Town, and hopefully she would no longer have any hang-ups over Dennis.

Dennis had seen to it that she was dealt with kindly by the authorities following her break-in at his apartment. Her father, Aaron, while passing along down the lane, had on numerous occasions thanked him for the kind help he had extended to his daughter.

### **THE OLD WEST INDIAN WOMAN**

In London, an old West Indian woman had returned too late to the pawnbrokers to retrieve her bangle. The proprietor, however, had given her the contact details that were left with him, and later Sonia received a letter forwarded from her mother. In the letter she had explained the sentimental value of the bangle, which her late husband had given her as a third year anniversary gift in 1925, and she would really appreciate buying it back. Also detailed in the letter was the same historical information that had been related to the pawnbroker. Finally, at the end of the letter she had signed her name as, Mrs Leonie Simpson.

As Sonia read the letter she was still wondering if the old family stories from her mother and uncle could really be be linked to this woman. But she dismissed it from her mind as there did not seem to be any apparent evidence forming a connection.

She was still thinking of how to reply to the woman's request, when she came across a letter left inside her granny's large King James family Bible. Sonia had only taken it down from the shelf as she was

# EPILOGUE

doing a little spring cleaning in the lounge, but then she had noticed the letter tucked in between the pages of Revelations. It was still in its opened overseas envelope addressed, not unsurprisingly, to her granny. But when she turned it over and saw who it had come from, Sonia at last realised she had discovered the connection. The letter was from the same woman, Mrs Leonie Simpson!

After sitting down and reading the letter, Sonia understood that granny Henni had been the only person Leonie had kept in touch with after being rejected by her own parents. It certainly was a lot of information uncovered that day. Firstly, Sonia learned that aunt Ruby and her brother, Gordon, were Leonie's siblings, whom she must also have been estranged to all these years. Secondly, the story of the bangles was complete without Leonie's even knowing it. And thirdly, Sonia also realised that Leonie was unaware of her aunt Miriam's death.

Sonia talked it over with Dennis, who was in agreement to them both taking a trip to London to meet Leonie, her long lost family member, before letting aunt Ruby know of the discovery. Leonie had not included a phone number, so Sonia replied to the letter, only informing her of granny's death and of their wish to meet and discuss with her about the bangle. Everything else they would wait to talk about face to face. A subsequent reply was soon received, asking questions about how they knew her aunt, and also inviting her and Dennis to her home anytime they were in London.

Well, when they eventually arrived at the humble terraced house, in a quiet cul-de-sac in central London, a smiling seventy eight year old woman greeted them at the door, and welcomed them in.

Sonia, eager to answer Leonie's questions, straight away began explaining their family connection. Leonie could not believe she was actually speaking with a family member after such a long time. Tears welled up in her eyes as she listened to what Sonia had to say about granny Henni and what she had told her about one of the bangle's past. Then she talked about them finding the other one, which Leonie had left in the pawnbroker's shop.

"And so, thanks to you, the two bangles are together once more," Sonia stated, giving Leonie a hug, "but we really would love to hear all about your side of the story."

# EPILOGUE

At that, Leonie proceeded to talk at length about her late husband, Rudyard Simpson, who had been an engineer on the Kingston to Spanish Town railway line when they first met in 1920; she was just 18, and he was 22. It all began one day when she was serving coffee to the railway workers, and he asked her what a beautiful girl like her was doing just serving coffee. Well, after smiling at his compliment that day, their friendship blossomed into love. Many times he would wait for her to finish work and then go strolling for a while by Parade, or King Street, before she had to take the Evening Star bus, back up country. The song **(42) "Strollin' On" (Maxi Priest)** summarised their feelings for each other in those early times.

Well, their relationship, which developed over two years, was something her parents, who were very anti-colonialist, vehemently opposed from the start. Her father, Marston Douglas, especially hated the colonial powers, whom he blamed for the death of his grandmother. Marston's father, Glenmore, had told him many times what had happened to his parents while they both worked on a local plantation estate. Glenmore's dad worked outside on the land as a labourer for banana cultivation, and his mother worked inside the big family house as a maid. Now, although at the time, slavery had been abolished for over 30 years, the low wages and atrocious working conditions was just like slavery in a different guise. It happened that Glenmore's mother had no choice but to continue working there when an outbreak of scarlet fever had infected two young children of the plantation owner. She soon found that she had got infected too while working in close proximity to them. Now, whereas the children survived due to having access to the best doctors and medicine, his mother sadly had to endure an agonizing death, being unable to afford the cost of treatment. The day before she died, Glenmore's father had run up to the big house begging for help, but was turned away; blasted by the owner for disturbing the game of cards he was having with his friends.

It was tales like this which had certainly influenced Leonie's father into hating the British colonial powers, and tarring anyone linked to it with the same brush, whether such hatred was warranted or not.

Leonie told her listeners how she had tried reasoning with her parents, saying that despite what had happened in the past, not everyone was the same. She had pleaded with them to give Rudyard a chance,

## EPILOGUE

but they would have none of it. Unknown to Leonie, her mother, Joslyn, had forgotten how it was that her love for Marston in the early days had made her sink to the level of agreeing to deceiving her father about her intended's financial status. It would certainly have saved all that trouble if she had just cast her mind back; but anti-colonialist feelings served to blind her to all reason. Hearing all of those arguments were her younger siblings, Ruby, and Gordon, who loved their older sister very much. Leonie loved them too, and did not want to leave them, but when her mother finally told her that it would be best for all concerned if she just forgot about Rudyard and find a nice Jamaican boy, Leonie knew she was left with no alternative...She was prepared to forsake everything for her one true love!!!

On the day that she ran away to get married in the registry office in Kingston, in 1922, only her mother's youngest of two sisters, aunt Miriam, who she was very close to, had secretly been in attendance; after leaving her husband, Rensford, in charge of their lovely two year old baby, George, for the day. Miriam was Leonie's favourite aunt who had accompanied her, three years earlier to seek work in Kingston. The railway terminus had advertised for workers, which sounded exciting and very different from the kind of work, if you could get work, in the village. The job she got was as a waitress in the terminus sandwich & coffee bar. She would need to catch the 6am Morning Star bus from her village to Kingston each day in order to be in work on time. Leonie loved the challenge it gave her, and her aunt had encouraged her too by telling her that 'life is what *you* make it,' and that she was sure she would succeed.

Well, a few months after their wedding, they left Jamaica because her husband's contract ended, and his next assignment was in Liverpool, England. That was where they settled for many years until an opportunity arose in 1950, when he was head-hunted to work on a new section of the London's underground tube network. He accepted the position, and they relocated to London. Despite wanting children, they had remained childless up to his sudden death from a heart attack in 1969; he was only seventy one.

She continued talking about how she had instructed her aunt not to give her address to anyone because she wanted a clean break from everyone, and was only concerned with her life with Rudyard, and no one else! But although she kept her distance, aunt

# EPILOGUE

Miriam had kept her informed over the years on what was going on with the family, including when her parents had passed away within two years of each other. Also, when her cousins George and Sandra were emigrating to England, she was made aware of that too, but did not feel the need to get in touch with them. Too many years of being away from the family had made her very self centred, and wrapped up in her world with Rudyard. And even though her parents had died, she did not think anyone would be interested in her after all those years anyway.

Leonie added that sometimes the communication with her aunt was by phone, other times by letter. About the time of granny Henni's death, her phone line had been disconnected, due to a period of financial hardship following some urgent roofing works on her house. This explained why she was unaware of her aunt's death. It dawned on her that something was wrong, when she did not receive a reply after six months since writing to her. Sonia's recent letter, informing her of her sad passing, had really come as a shock. But she was pleased to know that the funeral service had been so well supported.

When the time came for them to leave, Dennis

prepared to hand over his bangle to Leonie, which was what they had both decided to do beforehand. However, seeing what the bangles meant to them both, Leonie had changed her mind about wanting it back, insisting that they keep them both together; Leonie thought to herself that it would be just as they were originally meant to be with the princess.

They thanked her for allowing them to keep both bangles, then Sonia enquired about her research; she was intrigued to know how she had discovered so much about the bangle's history.

Leonie explained that it was really a coincidence that happened when she had accompanied her husband on a temporary work assignment, in West Africa, in 1947. One day while being escorted around a local village, her bangle was recognised by some older tribe-women, who kept the unwritten history of that village, passed on by oratory fashion through the generations. It was quite a story to hear about what had been a sentimental anniversary gift from her husband. And that was why she says she was at first reluctant to take it to the pawnbroker. Then as things turned out, she was unable to reclaim it as her funds were so low. But she said with a smile, "Everything's

# EPILOGUE

Ok now, and it's been so good to talk with you two lovely people."

Before leaving, Sonia invited her over for holiday as she had not been back to Jamaica since she left so many years before. She thanked them, but declined, saying it was too late in the day for her to start thinking about travelling again.

However, having members of her family there in her home that day did actually begin to soften her stance against getting in touch with her family. Indeed, she began dwelling on the idea of seeing them all again one day. Then she recalled something her aunt had whispered to her at the registry office in Kingston on her wedding day, "My dear, despite everything going on with your family, you should never burn your bridges behind you."

At last she realised, painfully too late, that what she had done was exactly that. A song she knew well, reminded her of her aunt's words, but she had never thought of applying it to herself until this time. It is called **(43) "Never Burn Your Bridges" (Don Campbell).**

Tears ran down her face when she thought about

her sister and brother, and what she had put them through over all those years. But she was determined to make changes.

Before returning to Jamaica, Sonia made sure that her mother and uncle were introduced to their long lost cousin, so she would no longer be without any family communications. Next, aunt Ruby and her brother were informed about their newly discovered big sister. Their happiness was beyond words when they got to speak with her on the phone, catching up on so much lost time. And, a few years later, when Hazel and George made their plans to return home to Jamaica, Leonie sold up and went home with them too, because when all is said and done, she concluded that home truly is where the heart is.

************

Don't miss part two

## LOVERS ROCK 2:
### Manhattan Skyline
**Get your copy on Amazon & Kindle**
*The music continues...*

# SONG LIST

| No | TITLE AND ARTIST | PAGE |
|---|---|---|
| 1 | It's You I Love  (The Techniques) | 20 |
| 2 | Play It Cool  (Alton Ellis) | 24 |
| 3 | The Real Thing  (Bitty Mclean) | 26 |
| 4 | Miss Wire Waist  (Carl Malcolm) | 35 |
| 5 | One Girl Too Late (Anthony 'Pure Silk' Brightly & Winsome) | 38 |
| 6 | Baby Please  (Peter Hunnigale) | 38 |
| 7 | Jealousy  (T.T. Ross) | 40 |
| 8 | Money In My Pocket  (Dennis Brown) | 41 |
| 9 | Country Living  (Sandra Cross) | 43 |
| 10 | I'm Still Waiting  (Delroy Wilson) | 45 |
| 11 | Crying Over You  (Ken Boothe) | 48 |
| 12 | Hurting On The Inside  (Sammy Levi) | 48 |
| 13 | All In The Game  (One Blood) | 48 |
| 14 | I Admire You  (Roland & Carolyn) | 52 |
| 15 | Never Gonna Give You Up  (Jean Adebambo) | 53 |
| 16 | If I Gave My Heart To You  (John Mclean) | 56 |

| No | TITLE AND ARTIST | PAGE |
|---|---|---|
| 17 | In The Living Years (Stevie Face) | 61 |
| 18 | Push Come To Shove (Freddie Mcgregor) | 64 |
| 19 | I'm so Sorry (Carroll Thompson) | 65 |
| 20 | Hello Stranger (Brown Sugar) | 69 |
| 21 | Breezin (Tradition) | 70 |
| 22 | Looking Over Love (Kofi) | 73 |
| 23 | Number 1 Girl (Barry Boom) | 80 |
| 24 | Kingston Town (Lord Creator) | 83 |
| 25 | In Loving You (Junior English) | 86 |
| 26 | Feel The Feeling (Bob Andy) | 95 |
| 27 | Still Waters (The Mighty Diamonds) | 95 |
| 28 | One In A Million (Sanchez) | 97 |
| 29 | After Tonight (Matumbi) | 98 |
| 30 | Satisfy My Soul (Bob Marley) | 102 |
| 31 | Tune In (Gregory Isaacs) | 109 |
| 32 | Keep It Like it Is (Louisa Marks) | 113 |
| 33 | I Know The Score (Frankie Paul) | 119 |

| No | TITLE AND ARTIST | PAGE |
|---|---|---|
| 34 | To love Someone (Paul Dawkins) | 132 |
| 35 | Love Is What You Make It Girl (Investigators) | 135 |
| 36 | In Love (Arema) | 143 |
| 37 | Baby I've Been Missing You (Bunny Maloney) | 144 |
| 38 | 6 Sixth Street (Jack Wilson) | 151 |
| 39 | Silly Games (Janet Kay) | 152 |
| 40 | Lovers Rock (Sugar Minott) | 153 |
| 41 | Rock Away (Beres Hammond) | 155 |
| 42 | Strollin' On (Maxi Priest) | 161 |
| 43 | Never Burn Your Bridges Behind You (Don Campbell) | 167 |

OTHER BOOKS BY THE AUTHOR

**Lovers Rock 2: Manhattan Skyline**
**Lovers Rock 3: Life Is What You Make It**
Susie Loves To Dream: Your Wish Can Come True
Susie Loves To Dream 2: The Lost Light Of Dreamland

## ABOUT THE AUTHOR

Hartley Hines lives in Wales, UK, and is an aspiring author who was born in Jamaica. His first book was a wonderful fairytale in his 'Susie Loves To Dream' series, subtitled 'Your Wish Can Come True,' and it has brought joy to all who have read it. And then came his epic saga, the 'Lovers Rock' series, of which this is the first instalment.

It seems that writing runs in the family; His brother, Steadman Hines, is the author of the very popular book 'My Jamaica,' that entertains you from beginning to end and is available to order on-line.

Printed in Great Britain
by Amazon